THE
MAKING OF AMERICA
SERIES

ROGERS
THE TOWN THE FRISCO BUILT

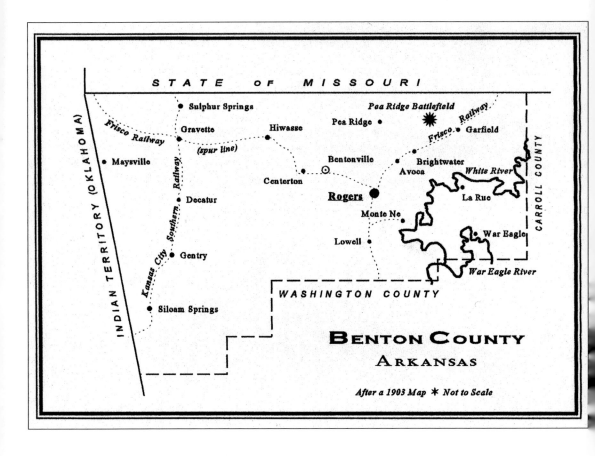

STATE OF MISSOURI

INDIAN TERRITORY (OKLAHOMA)

Frisco Railway

• Sulphur Springs

• Gravette

Hiwasse

(spur line)

• Maysville

Kansas City Southern Railway

• Decatur

Centerton

• Gentry

• Siloam Springs

Pea Ridge Battlefield

Pea Ridge •

Frisco Railway

• Garfield

Bentonville

Brightwater
Avoca

White River

Rogers ●

La Rue

Monte Ne •

• War Eagle

Lowell •

War Eagle River

CARROLL COUNTY

WASHINGTON COUNTY

BENTON COUNTY

ARKANSAS

After a 1903 Map ✳ *Not to Scale*

COVER: *A group of friends enjoy an afternoon drive to Diamond Springs, which was the principal source of water during the town's early years. Pictured, from left to right, are John Simon McLeod, Font Freeman, Wilida Freeman, Kate Freeman, and J.E. Felker.*

THE
MAKING OF AMERICA
SERIES

ROGERS
THE TOWN THE FRISCO BUILT

MARILYN H. COLLINS
ROGERS HISTORICAL MUSEUM

ARCADIA

First published 2002
Reprinted 2003

Published by Arcadia Publishing
an imprint of Tempus Publishing Inc.
Charleston SC, Chicago, Portsmouth NH, San Francisco

Printed in Great Britain

Library of Congress Catalog Card Number: 2002100842

For all general information contact Arcadia Publishing at:
Telephone 843-853-2070
Fax 843-853-0044
E-Mail sales@arcadiapublishing.com

For customer service and orders:
Toll-Free 1-888-313-2665

Visit us on the Internet at http://www.arcadiapublishing.com

This book is dedicated to my father and mother,
Elmer Simpson Harris and Ruby June Sager Harris.

CONTENTS

ACKNOWLEDGMENTS

A rich store of information from the people of Rogers provided the human drama for this book through stories, shared memories of the past, old photographs, and family mementos.

The Rogers Historical Museum has an extensive record of the collective history of Rogers including oral histories, photographs, documents, maps, and books. The staff has also written numerous brochures on the life and times of people in Rogers. This book would not have been possible without the assistance of Dr. Gaye Bland, director of the museum, who supported this effort from the beginning and has generously lent her knowledge and expertise to the project throughout. Allyn Lord, assistant director, knowledgeably checked each fact and editing detail. Marie Demeroukas, curator of collections, was very helpful in finding and selecting the best photographs possible from the museum's collection. Monte Harris, adult programs assistant, provided her knowledge of the downtown buildings and their use over the years. Pat Campbell and Anna Slawsky, office managers, also helped with the collection of data for the book.

Researchers and authors through the years have produced invaluable information upon which all future writers depend. Rogers is most fortunate to have a wealth of excellent newspaper reporting by the staff of the *Northwest Arkansas Morning News*, which later became the *Morning News*. These papers have been responsible for several excellent special editions on the history of Rogers and a continuum of articles about aspects of the town's history. The *Rogers Hometown News* and the *Benton County Daily Record* have also published many articles of interest about people and events of historic note in Rogers.

Other writers or publishers of local history include the following: J. Dickson Black, Opal Beck, Billie Jines, Barbara Easley, Verla McAnelly, Vera Key, Dorothy Ross, J. Wesley Sampier, Ruth Muse, Maggie Smith, Gary Townzen, and Casey Ward. The Benton County Historical Society publishes *The Benton County Pioneer* and reprinted *Goodspeed's 1889 History of Benton County, Arkansas.*

Many people offered photographs or materials for the book, and I am very grateful to each of them. They include Colonel Jerry Hiett, Opal Beck, Sam Woods, Gary Townzen, Sue Fleming, Casey Ward, Charles Musteen, Claudine Haskell, Beth and Carl Guest, Jan Oftedahl, Dick Trammel, Maurice Kolman, Mayor Steve Womack, Rhonda French, Emery and Ruth Davis, Mary Sue

Reagan, Betty Lynn Reagan, Betty and John Swearingen, Ethelmae Winkleman Craig, Alan Bland of the Army Corps of Engineers, Don Warden of the Siloam Springs Museum, Betty and Steve Goodman, John Applegate, Dell Christy Tyson, Linda Settles Jones, Faye Bottens Heins, Rick Williams, Ernestine Scott, Lorene Stephens, John Mack, Callison Funeral Home, Main Street Rogers, Tom Sager, Shirley Park, Dean Park, and Barbara Youree. Clifton Eoff and Bedford Camera and Video were very helpful in providing computer and photo development support. Artists John Creech and Andy Thomas were generous to offer me their original artwork for this book. Myra Moran, dealer and collector of rare books, provided an excellent selection of local, regional, and statewide books for this research.

Others not already mentioned who were particularly helpful in offering their input include Paul Dolle, Dr. Janie Darr, Sandra Fearman, Florence Felker, Doug Keller, Barbara Roberts, Chief Tim Keck, Jenny Harmon, Wendy Shumate, Raymond Burns, Tom Ginn, Johnny Jacobs, Barney Hayes, and Dale Webster.

I also appreciate my family who provided professional expertise as writers and editors as well as their personal encouragement: my sisters, Shirley Park and Barbara Youree; and my husband, Larry Collins. His indefatigable patience and positive attitude have been priceless. Dean Park, my brother-in-law, was especially helpful in providing material, photo reproduction, and computer advice. This book is dedicated to my parents who passed on to me their strong faith in God, belief in the power of prayer, love of family, and respect for the land.

A word of special thanks goes to Mark Berry of Arcadia Publishing for his faith in publishing a second book with me. I appreciate his wisdom and guidance.

The people of Rogers love a parade. Christmas, homecoming, celebrations for the return of servicemen—each brings out bands, majorettes, and streets lined with happy spectators. This 1930s parade marches down Poplar Street at the intersection of First and Second Streets. (Sam Wood.)

INTRODUCTION

Erwin Funk, longtime editor of the *Rogers Democrat*, was once asked to write the history of the Rogers Academy. Funk thought this "sounded like a harmless sort of undertaking that one might pound out in a few hours." All it took, after all, was just reading some old newspaper clippings and checking the memory of a few old timers! However, Funk's advice to prospective writers of history after getting into the project, as quoted in the *Rogers Daily News*, was "Maybe you have never tried to write about something that happened 50 years ago and wanted to be absolutely correct as to dates, names, initials, etc. And in the main, as to facts. My advice is: Don't!"

His own advice notwithstanding, Funk went on to compile his history, and this writer also forged ahead in spite of the odds against perfection. My purpose in writing *Rogers: The Town the Frisco Built* is to pay tribute to those men and women in Rogers who lived their lives productively, took care of their families, built churches and schools, started businesses, planted and harvested the fruit of the land, and held a faith in God and country that continues to guide us today. We pick up today where our ancestors left off and act our own parts as our talents and heritage require us.

Change through the years is, of course, inevitable. The explorers, then settlers, who were followed by merchants and farmers, radically changed this land first roamed by the American Indian. We are fortunate in Rogers that as progress has moved forward, sometimes at a rapid pace, we have kept our values and hometown spirit. New people coming to the area have supported what is good and added their own contributions to preservation in the midst of these changes.

Historic downtown Rogers is exceptional in today's business environment where the shops in many downtowns are often deserted or their original architecture covered with metal siding. Downtown Rogers has been preserved, not as a monument of the past, but as a vital living part of our present. The streets are still paved with brick and many original buildings still stand. The train—whose advent began it all—still runs down the track, whistle blaring, into town. Most of all the spirit of the people—generous by nature, caring of their neighbors, loving of community—continues today.

My hope is that each person who reads this book determines to leave an account of their life for their families and for posterity. It is, unfortunately, not possible within the scope of this book to speak to every person in Rogers or record each personal story. Therefore, if you call Rogers your home, I encourage you to add your notes to this book so that years from now your family will have a sense of the time and place that you held dear.

We are blessed to be a part of this heritage. It is through this book that I have attempted in a few brief pages to bring to life the laughter, tears, hard work, and innovative ideas of the people and framers of this town in which we all take pride—the City of Rogers.

—Marilyn H. Collins

Men at Winkleman's Produce load apples from a wagon to barrels for shipping. The leading industries in Benton County in the early 1900s were apple production and processing. (Rogers Historical Museum.)

FOREWORD

Although Rogers itself was founded in 1881, the history of this corner of Arkansas goes back to well before the Civil War. That history is filled with interesting people, significant events, and fascinating stories. In these pages you will meet some of the people and learn of the many events that have shaped the history of this community, which is truly at the heart of America. Here, the West, Midwest, and South meet, and influences from all three regions have shaped the unique heritage of our area.

We value that heritage, in part, because of the enormous changes taking place in our community. For the past three decades, the story of Rogers has been a story of phenomenal growth, a growth that has brought both opportunities and challenges. Through it all Rogers has managed to maintain a "small town" feel, a spirit of cooperation, and a strong sense of community.

The office and factory workers now moving to Rogers from across our nation and around the world actually share much in common with the frontiersmen who came here from Tennessee in the 1830s. They too are "pioneers" in search of a place to make a better life. They too are becoming part of the history of this community.

At the Rogers Historical Museum, we believe educating newcomers and youngsters about that history will help us to maintain a sense of community through the changes that are yet to come. This book will play a vital role in preserving the story of Rogers and in sharing it with newcomers, longtime residents, and visitors alike.

—Gaye K. Bland, Ph.D.
Director, Rogers Historical Museum

1. First Footprints on the Land

Rogers was first a hunting ground for American Indians seeking wild game and the fruits of nature's bounty. Later, European explorers traversed the land looking for riches and ways to develop new trade routes to the rest of the known world. However, the permanent settlement of the land was for the men and women who sought independence in a new world where they could make their home and start a community. In this place, our forefathers and mothers worked, married, had children, and started businesses—all before "Rogers" became its name.

We are part of all who went before us. We want to know who these people were, hear whispers of their dreams, and gain courage from their deeds of bravery and the independence by which they led their day-to-day lives. Why did they come? Why did some leave? What prompted others to stay and build businesses and raise families? Understanding this past helps clarify the present and offers a road map to the future. This is the story of Rogers—a story as much of people as it is of place.

Ancient people left us glimpses of their lives in bluff shelters where they lived high above the creeks that flowed beneath the ridges of the aged and worn Ozark Mountains. This Ozark Plateau, worn smooth through the ages, became part of the much larger Springfield Plateau that covers most of Northwest Arkansas, where Rogers is located today.

The nearby Boston Mountains are the most rugged section of this plateau. Early pioneers who followed simple Indian trails in oxcarts and modern-day folks who drove the winding roads through these mountains before the advent of Interstate 540 could testify to the challenge of travel and to the rare beauty in this area. The natural mountain barriers of the northwest and swamps in the southeast had a major influence on the path of settlement in Northwest Arkansas, and the difficult terrain of the Boston Mountains kept the frontier here much longer than elsewhere in the state where travel was easier.

Few clues remain from the native tribes who roamed this region more than 8,000 years B.C. These people are thought to have been hunters and gatherers who followed the seasons for berries, nuts, and other vegetation, and the animal migrations for meat and skins. Archeological digs have discovered much about this past at the bluff shelters where these American Indians lived in Northwest Arkansas. Spears and dart points indicate how they hunted wild game; axes, hammerstones, mortars, and net sinkers attest to their use of improved tools.

Imagine yourself part of the unspoiled nature of that time. You can almost hear the clash of stone on stone as men chiseled knives, stone scrapers, or spear points into being. These early bluff dwellers gathered grass and cane along the riverbanks to weave baskets and nets. They dug deep pits in the floors of their shelters and lined them with woven mats to hold and preserve food and seeds. Large rocks were used as a cover to protect the stores from predators.

Sheltered from rain and wind, the cliff dwellings stayed so dry that fragments of baskets and food remain there today. These unwritten records tell of daily life and even death—although still wanderers, these early people buried their dead. They made a "nest" of woven grass and laid the deceased on top in a fetal position before burial. The significance of this ritual is not known.

By the middle of the sixteenth century, the culture changed as more permanent villages were established. Natives planted crops and created pottery to hold their bounty. American Indians in this part of the Ozarks tempered their pottery with crushed mussel shells or bones mixed with clay for greater strength and sometimes decorated them after baking. The introduction of the bow and arrow was a major improvement in hunting game at a distance, and the points used on the arrow differed from the points used on earlier spears and knives. Villages in the Ozarks were smaller than in other areas in the state, but ample evidence remains of the early cultivation of corn, sunflowers, squash, and other plants

Village activity of early American Indians often took place along the banks of creeks and rivers. They caught fish in nets and, as weapons improved, were able to bring down game more quickly. (The University Museum/University of Arkansas.)

The Ozarks was not home to the Osage but was used as part of their hunting range. Over time, the natives moved or were moved to different parts of the state. Major habitats are indicated on this map. (Arkansas Archeological Survey.)

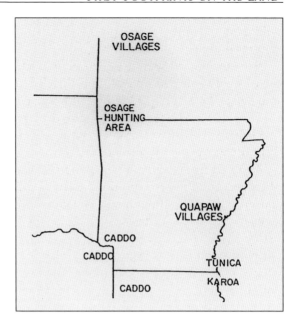

along creek banks. Walnuts, acorns, roots, and wild grape stems left other preserved traces of this culture.

Burial customs also changed, as bodies laid on top of the ground were covered with mounds of soil. The placement of numerous mounds in the same area is perhaps indicative of more social interaction in village life. Prior to the appearance of the first white explorers in Arkansas, knowledge about native life, religion, and customs is mostly interpreted from clues found in recovered artifacts.

Indian lore and legend combined with this documented scientific evidence provide us with some understanding of these people, but there is a common truism of how the early white settlers and the American Indians "recorded their history" in the following quote from *Folklore of Romantic Arkansas*. The white man said, "Where our grandfathers began, 'Once upon a time,' the Cherokee used the formula, 'This is what the old men told me when I was a boy.' " All of these stories, passed through oral tradition, carried a people's customs and beliefs and aided their ability to understand and survive the world around them.

The Spanish gave us the first written reports describing the lives of American Indians in this region. Hernando de Soto led the first expedition through Southeast Arkansas in 1541, and de Soto described the natives he encountered as "red devils." This name unfortunately influenced the imaginations of future pioneers from England and other European countries and, in part, defined their own approach to the American Indians.

When the French explorers Louis Jolliet and Jacques Marquette arrived in 1673, they found a very different native population, whose numbers had been decimated by influenza, smallpox, measles, mumps, and malaria contracted from the invading Europeans and for which the Indians had no natural immunity.

13

Early writings are still evident along the walls of cliff dwellers' caves at Eden's Bluff along the White River. Carl A. Starck points to some of the markings found in this typical rock shelter dwelling in the Ozarks. (Jerry Hiett.)

The first American Indians encountered by the French were called the "Arkansea," which meant "downstream people," as the tribe had moved down the Mississippi River into Arkansas. Later, Robert Cavalier, Sieur de la Salle would name these same people "Kapaha," or as they were later called, "Quapaw." Marquette also came upon the Osage in Northwest Arkansas during the 1673 expedition; however, these people probably did not live in the area but used it as part of their hunting range.

No record exists to indicate that early explorers came directly through what is present-day Rogers. However, the impact of their presence elsewhere in the state influenced migration patterns through the Ozarks. During the eighteenth century, increasing numbers of settlers heading westward pushed more and more American Indians across the Mississippi River into Arkansas. This eventually pressed the Cherokee into Osage hunting lands and fights over territorial rights ensued.

One of the motivating factors in President Thomas Jefferson's purchase of the Louisiana Territory in 1803 was to keep the peace. He paid $15 million (less than 4¢ per acre) to Napoleon Bonaparte for this land, and his intention was to re-settle all the eastern native tribes there. Those groups already living in the area had to move farther west. Through various moves, the Quapaw were forced to give up what remained of their diminishing land in Arkansas, and in 1824, they moved in among the Caddos, who occupied land in southwest Arkansas. The Quapaw were not particularly welcome in their new home, and starvation was rampant as the flooding Red River frequently destroyed crops.

Jefferson commissioned the first official American exploration of Arkansas in 1804–1805, and several other expeditions followed, usually tracing the major waterways in the state. Writer and geologist Henry R. Schoolcraft, however, did spend time in the Ozark Mountains. He described the people he found as mostly hunters isolated from outside influences. Few people lived in the territory, and only 1,062 were noted in the first United States census of 1810. These numbers reflected 924 white and 138 black people. Both federal and state censuses omitted a count of American Indians.

It was a natural disaster that actually initiated the first significant population increase in Arkansas. In 1811, the New Madrid earthquake caused the Mississippi River to flow backwards for over a mile and flood its banks. Trees were uprooted, mud and rock were thrown into the air, portions of the earth sank creating lakes, and, all in all, it was one of the worst earthquakes to take place in this country. The earthquake frightened the Cherokee, who feared the wrath of the "Great Spirit," into moving from their lands on the river to land between the Arkansas and White Rivers. In like manner, many white settlers thought that God had put a curse on the region and wanted to move away too. But Congress stepped in and offered landowners of ravaged ground an equal amount of land on public property in unaffected regions, encouraging settlers to move farther west into the state. Most who chose to resettle decided to homestead in the Ozarks of Arkansas and Missouri.

In 1819, President James Monroe signed a bill that made present-day Arkansas and part of Oklahoma into an official territory, and one that remained open to slavery. He also appointed James Miller, a New Hampshire resident and hero of the War of 1812, to be the first governor of the Arkansas Territory.

This newly formed territory soon caught the attention of William E. Woodruff, a New York printer, who realized that it was without a newspaper. Woodruff decided to pack his press and move, taking first a keelboat and then a flat-bottom boat to Arkansas Post, the territorial capital of Arkansas. The raftsmen who traveled with him were skeptical of his press, thinking it an "infernal engine spewing out bullets." After Woodruff set up shop in a two-room log cabin, he printed the first issue of the *Arkansas Gazette* on November 20, 1819.

Meanwhile, land disputes continued between the Cherokee and Osage Indians and were made worse by the appearance of white settlers bent on living in the same area. To help resolve this ongoing dispute, William L. Lovely, Cherokee agent to the Missouri Territory, purchased a portion of the Osage hunting grounds, which encompassed part of today's Benton County, and gave it to the Cherokee. The area later became known as Lovely County and included all or a part of nine other counties. All white settlers had to leave the area purchased by Lovely and many moved into what is now Oklahoma. The treaty of 1828 abolished Lovely County and the Cherokee were compensated for their Arkansas lands with land farther west. White settlers west of the Arkansas Territorial line then moved east while American Indians east of the line moved west into Indian Territory.

The state line and its shared border with Benton County were therefore set. Missouri's Thomas Hart Benton, for whom Benton County and Bentonville were named, however, argued against this placement of the state line; he had hoped to make Arkansas a larger and, thereby, stronger state. A forceful legislator, Senator Benton often spoke his mind and is quoted as once having said: "Mr. President, Sir, I never quarrel, Sir, but sometimes I fight, Sir, and when I fight, Sir, a funeral follows, Sir." Unfortunately, Benton's attempt to extend the borders of Arkansas failed despite his best efforts. Arkansas became a relatively small state by western standards and was deprived of large oil and other mineral resources. Additionally, American Indian settlements along the newly established western border became a barrier to further western expansion, and served to decrease the flow of pioneers—and their money—through the state. This final border designation, drawn due south from Missouri's western edge, cut off additional land that is now part of Oklahoma.

The border change affected settlers such as Adam Batie, thought to be the first white settler in Benton County following the 1828 treaty allowing white men into the area. Prior to that, Batie had settled on the west side of Benton County but was forced to leave, as it was Indian land at that time. His move back into Arkansas was the first step in the ensuing white settlement of Benton County.

However, conflict over land between the American Indians and white settlers was still unsettled. Although declared illegal by the Supreme Court, a forced western migration of American Indians from the east was authorized by President Andrew Jackson, and the trek that made its way through Northwest Arkansas was sorrowful and cruel. Thousands died en route from exposure and the lack of adequate or edible food. Though not all Indians were without means—some rode

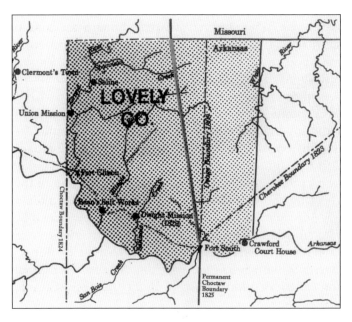

William Lovely purchased land from the Osage as a means of settling land disputes between them and the Cherokee people. The designated area was called Lovely County, and only Cherokees were allowed to live there. White settlers were not permitted in the area until the treaty of 1828 abolished Lovely County. (Siloam Springs Museum.)

Senator Thomas Hart Benton (1782–1858) fought hard to extend the borders of Arkansas so the state could better compete with the resources of oil and other minerals held by larger western states. (Library of Congress Photoduplication Service.)

on horseback or in fine carriages—most walked, scantily clad and barefoot, on muddy and sometimes frozen ground. The elderly and the very young were least able to survive. Those natives that did escape migration often listed themselves as "Black Dutch," "Spanish," "Creole," or "Black" to avoid detection.

The route, aptly named the "Trail of Tears," was actually several "trails" used by different groups as they pushed west. Between 1831 and 1839, Arkansas was part of the route for thousands of natives moving to the Indian Territory from other states. These trails later served as pathways used by European immigrants, as well as the routes taken by military roads, railroad tracks, early rude roads, and, eventually, asphalt highways—each reflecting the evolving history of the state.

Indian travel through local villages in the 1830s was also not without conflict. An incident in Fayetteville, recorded in *A History of Washington County* and later related in the *Northwest Arkansas Times*, involved a fight to the death between a Cherokee man and Willis Wallace, a local resident. Some of the natives camping near Fayetteville crowded into a local liquor store and much shouting and scuffling followed. But it was not until nightfall, when a drunken white man was said to have insulted a Cherokee woman, that violence broke out. Wallace fatally stabbed one of the natives. A crowd soon gathered, but Wallace went into hiding and the Indians withdrew. The case went to trial, but Wallace was found not guilty.

The mass movement of American Indians west of the Arkansas border ended most of the major land struggles in Arkansas. From time to time, however, minor incidents continued to occur as both American Indians and settlers challenged the border authority's enforcement of regulations that kept Indians on the west side and white settlers on east side of the state line.

17

2. Early Settlers to Northwest Arkansas

While the first explorers of the New World were often bent on finding gold or trade routes to the rich markets of Europe and the Orient, the earliest white settlers made the hazardous voyage across the Atlantic Ocean to seek economic opportunity and a greater freedom to live and express their beliefs. Following the American Revolution, the lure of the newly opened American Indian lands drew more settlers westward. Later, the thirst for gold would again sing its siren song and draw speculators west through Arkansas on their way to quick fortune in California.

Many descendants of the first settlers in Benton County, however, never left and continue to live on their family lands or in nearby towns. These great-great-grandchildren display their forefathers' enterprising spirit, interest in education, and strong religious beliefs, as evidenced by the county's continued economic growth, ever increasing number of schools, and many churches.

At the time when Adam Batie was settling on the western side of Benton County near Maysville in 1829, William Reddick and his family were putting down roots near Elkhorn on the eastern side of the county. Between 1830 and 1832, Jacob Roller joined other members of the Roller family on Roller Ridge near Pea Ridge; Enoch Trott, J. Wade Sikes, and Reverend Jasper Reddick also settled near Pea Ridge. Many other early names of note in Northwest Arkansas are cited in *The History of Benton County* by J. Dickson Black and in *Goodspeed's 1889 History of Benton County, Arkansas*. The following is only a partial list of those individuals who played a role in the early days of settlement: James Jackson, Simon Sager, Christian Christopher Sager, Daniel Ask, Jacob Forgey, Henning Pace, Henry Ford, George P. Wallace, James S. Black, John B. Dickson, David McKissick, Reverend James Harris, Colonel Hugh A. Anderson, Henry R. Austin, Young Abercrombie, Stephen Coose, John Scennett, David Walker, and Charles W. Rice. Some of the early settlers in the War Eagle area included John B. Kirk, Julius Kirk, Absalom Thomas, Henry Taber, Lewis Russell, Sylvanus and Catherine Blackburn, Josiah Blackburn, Matthew Brewer, and Peter Van Winkle.

To survive, these settlers brought with them the skills necessary to become successful farmers, builders, millers, blacksmiths, cabinetmakers, surveyors, hunters, teachers, and preachers. Women brought needed domestic abilities and passed down handcrafted quilts, needlework, and clothing patterns to the next generation. The day-to-day survival of these stalwart people depended on knowing how to preserve foods by drying and curing, grinding corn or wheat for baking, using available skin and fur from animals to make clothes and footwear, and finding simple cures for ailments from the plants around them.

Some jobs were more odious than others. For instance, early settlers rendered fat for candles or for making lye soap with wood ashes and old grease. In *Arkansas Celebration Cookbook: 150 Years of Ozark Cookin'*, a recipe for making lye soap includes the following directions, probably gained from unpleasant personal experience: "hold your breath, turn away to breathe, and don't inhale the vapor" while stirring the bubbling ingredients with a wooden paddle in a large cooking pot. The curative power of lye soap made it worth the discomfort. It purported to take the itching out of chigger bites and poison ivy, clear up skin and scalp problems, as well as clean clothes.

Sources of water in Northwest Arkansas played a powerful role in developing permanent settlements, and Benton County was blessed with an abundant supply of pure water that drew families and livestock owners to the area. Equally important, channeled river water made gristmills, water-powered woodworking shops, and sawmills possible. Virgin timber was the second source of emerging enterprise. Logs were floated or hauled out of the woods and made into usable lumber or furniture at the sawmills.

Many early settlers came to Northwest Arkansas from Tennessee, North Carolina, Kentucky, Virginia, Georgia, and Missouri. The faces in this drawing reflect the hardships they encountered. (Dover Publications.)

19

Millwrights were among the first settlers in Benton County. Sylvanus and Catherine Blackburn arrived during the fall of 1832, and after spending some time in the home of John Fitzgerald near Lowell, Blackburn moved his family to the War Eagle River bottom. The first mill operation run by the Blackburns was probably a pestle mill. In this operation, the top of a stump was burned to form a hollow where corn could be placed. A device resembling a teeter-totter then ground the corn with an up-and-down motion made by a person pressing on each end of the pole. Flour from the first batches was often "flavored" with charred pieces of stump. Later, a dam of rocks and logs was constructed and waterpower was used to grind the grain on a burrstone. Isaac and Levi Borne, bear hunters living upstream from the mill, were perhaps its typical customers, supplementing their food supply of meat with a small garden of corn that they had ground at the Blackburn mill. The mill only ran when there was enough wheat or corn to keep it busy all day. In 1838, a flood washed away this early mill, but the Blackburns quickly rebuilt, improving the mill by adding a sawmill, carpentry shop, and a blacksmith shop. During the Civil War, the Confederates burned the structures, but the Blackburns rebuilt the mill in 1873.

In 1851, Peter Van Winkle and his family established their mill in a narrow valley along the War Eagle. It became the largest of its kind in the region and supplied lumber for many of the buildings in the town of Rogers, as well as for

Peter Van Winkle and his family were some of the earliest arrivals in the county. They settled near War Eagle and built one of the largest mills in the area. (Rogers Historical Museum/Marilyn Hicks.)

U.S. Senator J.A.C. Blackburn, a son of early millers, married Peter Van Winkle's daughter Ellen. (Jerry Hiett.)

"Old Main" on the Arkansas Industrial University campus (later the University of Arkansas) and the Benton County Courthouse. Van Winkle also built a cabinet shop and flour mill, which were first powered by oxen and later with a steam-powered saw. Van Winkle was instrumental in the economic growth of the county in the late 1860s, and his daughter Ellen married the Blackburns' son J.A.C. Blackburn, who later worked for Van Winkle and, in 1884, succeeded him as proprietor of the mill. The Van Winkle business continued to prosper, and Blackburn became known in the area as "the lumber king."

German immigrants, hoping to escape the turmoil and economic discontent of their native land by coming to America, also built their businesses around lumber. Simon Sager and his brother Christian Christopher Sager, for instance, were mainly cabinetmakers and millers. Christian Sager, with his cousin Frederick Green, settled near Prairie Creek, where they ran a water-powered cabinet shop, mill, and store. The ledger from their store and examples of the Sager furniture can be seen at the Rogers Historical Museum and the Siloam Springs Museum. (Henry, a third Sager brother, migrated as far as Westport, Missouri and, among other things, helped build the Windwagon—a wagon with sails—designed to sail across the prairies at great speed.)

Several grist and lumber mills were operating in the area during the 1800s including the War Eagle mill, Hawkins mill, Johnson mill, Sager mill, Cave Springs mill, Cane Hill mill, S.S. Williams mill, Wesley mill, and the Van Winkle mill. By 1860, there were 97 gristmills in Arkansas. Not only did these and other early mills in Benton County help to build the economy, but enterprising owners often became leading citizens in their communities as educators and political leaders.

Mills along the rivers and creeks, such as this one at War Eagle, ground corn and grain or cut limber. This mill, rebuilt in 1973 on the original site, hosts one of the largest craft fairs in the Ozarks. (Jerry Hiett.)

Arkansas rivers provided the earliest means of transportation through the state—first for American Indians, then explorers, and later settlers. Large, bulky items could be moved much more easily on water than hauled over land. Steamboat travel began as early as 1831 and reached as far as Batesville on the White River. Such travel was not always the romantic picture sometimes imagined. Boats often did not reach their destination on schedule because of low water levels, and time was lost waiting for rivers to rise. Also, fallen trees and rocks could snag a boat and result in the loss of cargo and occasionally even life. But the most dangerous part of travel by steamboat was the temperamental nature of the boilers. A report in the December 9, 1840, edition of the *Arkansas Gazette* tells of a steamboat disaster on the Arkansas River near Morrilton and provides graphic detail of this danger.

> She had not been at the landing more than 10 minutes before her boilers exploded, sweeping right and left, from midship forward, every part from the guards up. One boiler was thrown into the river; the other on shore, making the most dreadful havoc of human life that can be imagined. One man was thrown up in the air 200 feet and fell in the town some distance from the river's bank; seventeen other persons were killed . . . From nine to 14 persons known to have been on board are missing; 18 or 20 persons are severely injured, some burned, some scalded, others with broken legs, heads and arms presenting, as we are informed by an eye witness, a scene too horrid for description.

Travel by land, especially across the Boston Mountains, was also arduous. The early trails left by hunters, generously labeled "roads," were only barely cleared. Trees were cut, but often the stumps remained, making travel a teeth-jarring experience for people riding in a wagon or oxcart.

The number of settlers in the Ozarks increased dramatically over the next few years. The population of "Arkansas" grew from 1,062 in the 1810 census to 14,255 in 1820, to 30,388 in 1830, and to 52,241 by 1835 (42,302 white and 9,936 black; American Indians were still not included in the census). By 1850, the population numbered 209,899 of which 162,109 were white and 47,708 were slaves. The 1860 census for Benton County listed 9,285 as the total population including "8,905 white, 385 Negro, and 16 Indian." Many of these original families to Benton County came from earlier pioneer families who first settled in Tennessee, North Carolina, Kentucky, Virginia, Georgia, or Missouri.

Few of the families living in the mountainous part of Arkansas Territory had slaves. Although slaves were used in the Van Winkle mill and elsewhere, small farms and the lack of large industry kept the need for slaves very low. However, when the case for statehood arose in 1836, Arkansas applied to the Union as a slave state. In preparation for this admission, Arkansas held a constitutional convention in Little Rock on January 4, 1836. Each slave state applying for admission had to be offset with an incoming free state to keep a balance of power in Congress. Michigan entered the Union as a free state as Arkansas entered as a

The mill at Cave Springs was another mill in a line that dotted the banks of local creeks. (Sam Wood.)

Simon Sager, a German immigrant, built his cabin at Siloam Springs in 1837. The cabin stands today on the John Brown University campus. (Marilyn Collins.)

slave state. Six months later on June 15, 1836, President Andrew Jackson signed the bill giving Arkansas statehood. The Arkansas Slave Code, passed in 1837, provided a framework dictating what owners could and could not do and what slaves could and could not do. A former slave expressed the harshness of life this way: "You worked from the time you could see until the time you couldn't see."

Eighteen thirty-six was a stellar year for Arkansas and for the people in Benton County. Today's Benton County was once a part of Carroll County, and when Washington County was organized in 1828, it encompassed all of what is today Benton County, as well as parts of Carroll and Madison Counties. Benton County became a county in its own right, and the 34th in Arkansas, in 1836, and on that same day, the Territory became the 25th state admitted into the Union. The governor appointed the first county officials who would serve until an election could be held. For Benton County, these men were George P. Wallace, county judge; John B. Dickson, county clerk; Gideon G. Pace, sheriff; Henry C. Hastings, treasurer; Henry Ford, coroner; and Alexander McKissick, surveyor.

A committee was soon formed to select a county seat, and in November 1837, the committee filed its report, stating that "duly considering its situation, the donations offered, and its eligibility for a county seat, more advantages and conveniences than any other situation . . . . have named and called said town Bentonville." Also named for Missouri Senator Thomas Hart Benton, Bentonville became the county seat.

Education was another great concern of county leaders. When Arkansas became a state, a small portion of every township was set aside to fund education. This land was leased or sold and the proceeds used to support education efforts. This was a faulty system, however, that was rescinded in 1846. Education funding was then left to the discretion of the local counties to raise and administer. With very little money for education, nearly a quarter of Arkansas's population in the mid-nineteenth century could neither read nor write.

Children, especially poor children, depended heavily on the often-limited education of their parents or on the sometimes-limited education of their teacher, if they were fortunate enough to attend a school. Early schools enrolled students through a subscription system, so children unable to pay were left out. Homes and one-room log cabins served as classrooms for schools, which were typically in session just three months during the year—although the school year could be extended if the community had additional money to pay a teacher. Teachers, in any event, were poorly paid.

The mid-1800s saw difficult economic times in Arkansas. Both the State Bank and the Real Estate Bank failed in 1842. In 1844, the state outlawed banks, and there were no commercial banks in Arkansas from that time until after the Civil War. This action was a particular hardship for farmers and small businessmen who

Children played simple games in the schoolyard during recess. Liberty School is typical of the one- and two-room schoolhouses that dotted the county prior to the late 1920s. (Rogers Historical Museum.)

depended heavily on credit. No loans were available, which further depressed the economy and dramatically limited growth.

The state's population also decreased as hard times helped drive recruits to the war with Mexico (1846) and people enchanted by the promise of gold to California. Fort Smith, Van Buren, Fayetteville, and the Rogers area became major conduits for those heading west during the gold rush of 1849. One wagon a day loaded with prospectors soon became 20 wagons a day. As stated in *America Moves West*, gold fever created a "mad mining rush during which sailors deserted their ships, cattle tenders left their herds, farmers abandoned their plows, and merchants closed their stores." This exodus became a drain not only of people but also of money. The state even attempted to stem this outward flow of resources by not improving roads.

With much of the country's population heading west, the need for greater and faster methods of communication became evident. In 1853, Congress granted the first Arkansas railroad charter, and in 1860, the first telegraph line in the state was built from Memphis to Little Rock.

In 1857, Congress also decided to establish a mail route across the country. Naturally, there was a great deal of controversy over which towns the route would cross—every community wanted to bring prosperity their way. The Postmaster General was given the chore of selecting the mail routes and the company that would be charged with carrying the mail. The first temporary contract went to Jim Birch; his service, however, was so slow (due in part to his use of mules) that it soon became known as the "Jackass Line." Nine more bids were then let, and the contract went to John Butterfield, who for $600,000 a year would provide regular stagecoach service.

A year later, in 1858, the Butterfield Overland Mail Company made its first run with 141 stations in place and about 1,200 horses and 600 mules to pull the coaches. John Butterfield and other notables rode on the first trip in a coach driven by his son. Famous stops in and near the present location of Rogers were Elkhorn Tavern in Pea Ridge, Callahan Tavern in Rogers, and Fitzgerald's Station in Shiloh (Springdale). The hotel and stage stops in Fayetteville were also important, as John Butterfield owned both.

Elkhorn Tavern was never listed as an official station but was a popular stop along the way, and three and a half years later, in March 1862, the tavern played a role in the Civil War battle at Pea Ridge. (Elkhorn Tavern has been restored and is now open to visitors at the Pea Ridge National Military Park in Pea Ridge.) Just 10 miles south of the tavern was an official mail stop in Rogers at Callahan's Tavern, located on the Old Wire Road near East Spruce Street, later the site of the Wilmoth Sanitarium and currently the Office of Human Concern.

Two routes ran weekly from St. Louis. One went through Memphis and the other went through Rogers to Fort Smith and on to San Francisco. Passengers paid $200 going and $100 coming back, while short-trip riders paid 10¢ a mile. Mail riders picked up mail from designated sites or from fence "posts" along the road where people left their mail or took it to a collection point for the stage.

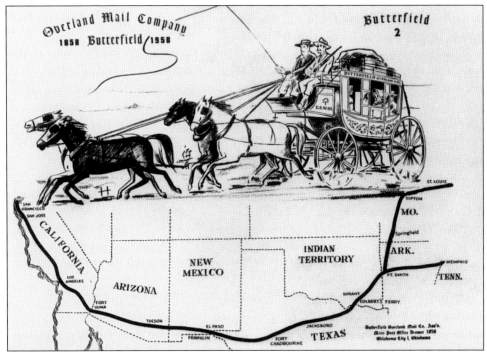

Passengers on the Butterfield Overland stage made their first official stop in Arkansas at Callahan's Tavern in Rogers. The Butterfield Overland Mail Route went from St. Louis to San Francisco. (Rogers Historical Museum.)

As roads became more passable, stagecoach travel became the most common form of cross-country transportation prior to the railroads. But stagecoach travelers often had harrowing tales to tell. Passengers were shaken about and sometimes made to walk over treacherous ground or up hilly inclines to lighten the load for the horses. Although some stops provided reasonable accommodations, overnight stays often meant sleeping in the open on the ground or staying in filthy hovels. Some accommodations were only one- or two-room cabins that did not allow for separate sleeping spaces. Food consisted of "dirty bread, tough chicken with lard poured over them for butter and no sugar for coffee," reported a stage passenger going from Little Rock to Fort Smith. The report continued, "They say we must eat our peck of dirt before we die. I think in Arkansas, we . . . ate it all at once."

On leaving the plateau of the stations in Benton and Washington Counties, passengers endured a somewhat frightening ride. According to one passenger's report in *Butterfield Run Through the Ozarks*, "I might say our road was steep, rugged, jagged, rough, and mountainous . . . and then wish for some more expressive words in the language. . . . The wiry, light little animals tugged and pulled as if they would tear themselves to pieces and our heavy wagon bounded along the crags as it if would be shaken in pieces every minute, and ourselves disemboweled on the spot." The only relief to these passengers was the spectacular beauty of the Boston Mountains.

The route of the Butterfield Overland Stage became the forerunner of the telegraph and later the railroad through Rogers. As new means of communication grew more advantageous both to commerce and the traveler, the stagecoach faded into the past. However, the high adventure, danger, both real and perceived, and the excitement of riches farther west experienced by those early travelers still evoke a thrill in our imagination today. A passage in *American Moves West* nostalgically states the following:

> Gone were the lumbering oxcart, the covered wagon, the long dangerous trip across the plains, the nightly stop with its gleaming campfire. Gone were the jolting stage, the periodic station, the driver with his cracking whip. Gone were the trapper, the trader, the hunter, and the explorer. In their places appeared the modern and efficient, but impersonal, steam locomotive. The result was eventually a transformation in the characteristics and state of mind of the West.

Dennis Callahan built the tavern and stage stop along Callahan Springs on the first "farm-to-market" road from Fayetteville, Arkansas, to Springfield, Missouri. Although most of the original tavern was destroyed during the Civil War, the site has been home to other enterprises such as the Office of Human Concern. (Marilyn Collins.)

3. VOICES OF WAR

By 1860, Northwest Arkansas was beginning to develop and establish better connections to the rest of the country. Improved roadways, more navigable waterways, and the newly opened Butterfield Overland Stage allowed people to travel more safely, and communication by mail to the East and West Coast was now possible. Telegraph lines, which followed the route between St. Louis and Fayetteville, were open between St. Louis and Fayetteville and between Memphis and Little Rock.

However, the distant rumblings of war foretold the horror to come. The fledgling economy in Northwest Arkansas was put on hold as debates on secession and the coming war dominated most thought. The land that was gained as the result of the Mexican War created a greater controversy within the United States as debate erupted over whether the newly acquired land would be accepted as a slave or free state.

Many people in Northwest Arkansas felt that the country should maintain its union. But they also sympathized with the feelings of their neighbors in the cotton counties in the southern and eastern part of the state who wanted Arkansas to secede. With some ambivalence, delegates met at the state convention in Little Rock on February 18, 1861, less than a month before Abraham Lincoln made his inaugural address as President. The Unionists outnumbered the Secessionists, and the vote to secede was defeated with the caveat that if any of the six Southern states that had already seceded from the Union were attacked, Arkansas would enter the conflict on the side of the South. The legislature then decided to let the people vote on secession, and a vote was set for August 5, 1861.

Circumstances preempted this action when, on April 12, Confederate forces fired on the Federal troops at Fort Sumter in Charleston, South Carolina. As a consequence of this action, President Lincoln called on Governor Henry M. Rector of Arkansas to provide troops to support the Union's response. The governor refused, believing that the citizens of Arkansas were "insulted" by such a request.

The legislature met again on May 6 for another vote on secession, and the first vote was reversed with 65 for secession to just 5 against. Four of the negative votes were later changed to agree with the majority. Only the Unionist delegate from Madison County did not change his vote. On May 20, 1861, Arkansas joined the Confederacy and sent two senators and four representatives to the Confederate Congress.

There were many names for this conflict depending on with which side the speaker was aligned: "Civil War," "War Between the States," "War of the Rebellion," "War for Southern Independence," "The Great Unpleasantness," and so forth. Regardless of the name used, allegiances and sentiments often differed even among family members. This epic struggle pitted friend against friend, family against family, and the toll in lives was enormous. The war not only turned white settlers against one another but also American Indians, who participated in the conflict on both sides. Even religious denominations added "North" and "South" to their names. The war had a far-reaching effect on politics and wealth in Northwest Arkansas, and it continues to evoke strong feelings even today.

A new state constitution was approved by the Arkansas Secession Convention on June 1, 1861, and the preamble asserted its purpose: "to continue ourselves as a free and independent State," to secure for its citizens the right of life, liberty, property, and the pursuit of happiness. "Property," at that time, included the right of ownership of slaves. The body of the constitution also clearly stated that "the union now subsisting between the State of Arkansas and the other states, under the name of the United States of America, is hereby forever dissolved."

Before the legislature adjourned, a military board was appointed and given full military authority, subject only to the convention and legislative acts. In addition, an eastern commander and western commander were appointed for the Confederates. Concern that American Indian attacks on Arkansas, Louisiana, and Texas would detract from the war effort led to the appointment of Albert Pike as commissioner to the Choctaw and Cherokee tribes. Pike was considered a friend by the Indians and successfully negotiated treaties between the Confederate States and tribes living to the west of Arkansas. Jefferson Davis later put Pike in charge of all tribes in the Indian Territory. Pike successfully recruited the natives—some were slave owners themselves—to take the side of the Confederacy, but he later encountered problems when he had to break his policy of letting American Indian soldiers fight only on their own lands. Ordered to bring natives to Pea Ridge to participate in the conflict, he was blamed when scalping incidents were attributed to the Indians.

Benton County men played an important role in conflicts west of the Mississippi. Company A of the Fifteenth Arkansas Regiment led by Captain J.H. Hobbs was organized in the summer of 1861. Soon Companies F and G were formed under the leadership of Captain William Thompson and Captain J.M. Richards, respectively. All in all, there were 11 companies raised in Benton County. Other groups followed, totaling 1,100 men plus hundreds more who joined as recruits.

Arkansas sons were initiated into their first conflict at Wilson's Creek, also called Oak Hill, near Springfield, Missouri, in August 1861. Four hundred and twelve of the 1,218 Confederate losses at this battle were Arkansas men. Though Missouri was a slave state, there was strong sentiment for the Union among its citizens, and Arkansas wanted to protect itself from Northern invasion, especially through Missouri. General Ben McCulloch of Texas was sent to help protect the northern border of Arkansas from attack, and he joined his forces with those of General Sterling Price. When Missouri voted not to secede, McCulloch and Price gathered Confederate supporters in Missouri and doubled the 5,000 Arkansas troops they already commanded. The Confederates prevailed over the Federal forces led by General Nathaniel Lyon at Wilson's Creek, and Lyon was killed during the battle.

The first action to take place on Benton County soil occurred in February 1862, near Avoca, on the farm of Reverend J. Dunagin. General Samuel Curtis, with his Federal forces, pursued the Confederates led by General Price as he returned from Missouri to rejoin General McCulloch in Arkansas. Not liking this treatment, Price's rear guard commander, General James S. Rains, set up an ambush leading the Federal forces into what looked like an easy victory over a small group of unprotected Confederate troops. Confederate soldiers hidden along the Union approach cut down the charge. In retaliation, the Federal troops burned their first house in Benton County—the home of Reverend Dunagin. This type of action typified many battles during the war, in which neither side was willing to leave the spoils of war to the other. Homes were burned, as were crops still in the field, stored in barns, or on docks awaiting shipment.

The Confederate army, including troops from Arkansas, prevailed at Wilson's Creek (or Oak Hill, as it was also known) near Springfield, Missouri. Troops had to carry water from the creek up to this house, which they used as their headquarters. (Marilyn Collins.)

31

There was some disagreement between the two Confederate generals as to the disposition of their forces. General McCulloch did not have much faith in General Price and his troops from Missouri. To resolve the situation, President Jefferson C. Davis set up the Trans-Mississippi Department 2, which included Western Arkansas, Indian Territory, Missouri, and part of Louisiana. ("Trans-Mississippi" referred to the states west of the Mississippi River.) General Van Dorn was appointed overall commander of the combined forces to resolve the differences between McCullough and Price.

The Mississippi River was an important link from the waterways of the north and east to the Arkansas River to the west and served as a conduit of men and supplies to the Confederacy. It was important to both Union and Confederate armies to gain and hold control of the river. From the end of February until March 6, 1862, troop movements in Northwest Arkansas were frequent as each side maneuvered for the stronger position.

Knowing the value of Arkansas as a border state to the Mississippi River, General Van Dorn, hoping for a strategic victory, positioned his troops along Pea Ridge near Lee Town during the night of March 6, 1862, and prepared for a morning attack on the Union army under the leadership of General Curtis. Van Dorn hoped not only to launch a surprise attack but also to cut off the Union's communication and supply route. A Confederate victory at Pea Ridge would allow the Southern army to later attack General Grant from the rear, thus

Actors fire this field piece at Pea Ridge National Military Park to demonstrate for onlookers what the noise of battle was like. Imagine the sound of this one cannon, magnified many times, which the soldiers on both sides endured. (Marilyn Collins.)

maintaining control of the Mississippi River along the Arkansas and Tennessee border. Van Dorn also wanted to conquer Missouri for the Confederacy.

Since military encampments were often located along creek banks where existing water-powered mills could be used to help supply food for soldiers and their animals, the land in and around Rogers played an important role in this battle. Troops maneuvered along the Osage River, at Cross Hollows, and in the towns of Bentonville and Fayetteville; Rogers was strategically located as it straddled the two major routes used by forces from both sides. (Accounts of these activities deserve full detail that is beyond the scope of this book. Local information can be found at the Pea Ridge National Military Park visitor's center and museums in both Benton and Washington Counties.)

The night of March 6 prefaced the most important battle fought in Arkansas: the Battle of Pea Ridge, or Elkhorn Tavern. For two days, on March 7 and 8, a bloody battle raged with the advantage first going to the Confederates and then to the Federals. Victory and perceived victory changed sides several times during the conflict because intelligence information was sketchy, and both sides thought the other had the larger numbers and more ammunition.

The Confederates entered into the battle already tired, having spent the previous night on a march made more difficult by felled trees and other obstacles laid in the way by Union troops. The Confederate troops finished their last day of marching with no food and only the water they could find on the battlefield.

Hunt P. Wilson, who fought in the Battle of Pea Ridge, painted a firsthand account of the conflict taking place near Elkhorn Tavern as depicted on this plaque at the Pea Ridge National Military Park.

The men "slept on their hands" in what little time they had to rest. By the end of the battle, the Confederates, who were out of ammunition, fought with rocks. Each side lost over a thousand men on the battlefield and many more would die from wounds received during the fighting.

General Van Dorn's men finally left the field of battle and, after traveling a few miles, made camp, rested, and began to take care of their wounded. They later retreated over the Boston Mountains to Van Buren, which was a major supply headquarters for the Confederate army. General Curtis of the Federal army did not pursue but also made camp and cared for his wounded. Much more than just a victory was gained by Union forces and much more lost by Confederate forces at the Battle of Pea Ridge, later known as the "Gettysburg of the West." Missouri was saved for the Union, shifting the location and outcome of future conflicts in favor of the Federals.

Where guns once roared and the cries of the dying filled the air, these fields now lie silent, the quiet broken only by the call of a bird or the sound of a carload of visitors to the battle site, which was established as a national park in 1960. Standing quietly or walking over the land dampened by the blood of kith and kin provides visitors with a sense of the devastation of the struggle and all that was won and lost here.

Elkhorn Tavern, held at different times by both the Federals and the Confederates during the battle, still stands today. For many years, elk horns adorned the building facade. Stolen by Union troops following the war and taken

The fields are quiet today as visitors walk the battleground at Pea Ridge. However, in our imagination, guns still roar and the shouts of men ring out across the fields. (Marilyn Collins.)

Elkhorn Tavern served as the headquarters and a field hospital during the Battle of Pea Ridge. (Rogers Historical Museum.)

to New York, the horns were later bought and returned to the tavern. Built by William Reddick, the tavern was later sold to a Mr. Cox who lived in the tavern with his family. The story goes that during the battle, the Cox family hid beneath the tavern floorboards for safety. In horror, they watched the blood of the wounded drip through the floor and into their hiding place.

War brings out the best and the worst in people. Aside from the organized battle strategies in which men are wounded and killed, another kind of violence was rampaging through the countryside as murderers, thieves, and other evildoers preyed on the people in Benton County. Homes were pillaged, fences and barns burned, people were killed and sometimes even hung for their money or for information. Many families told personal stories of loss and mistreatment. Other battles and skirmishes throughout the state and the Ozarks followed. In Washington County, Fayetteville was captured on July 14, 1862, followed in early December by the Battle of Prairie Grove near that city.

In May 1865, the Arkansas Confederate State Government ended; Congress established military law in the state in 1866. On June 22, 1868, Arkansas was readmitted into the Union under the controversial program of Reconstruction, which ended when the voters ratified a new state constitution and elected a slate of Democrats to office in 1874. The land's wounds were beginning to heal and the hardiness that had brought the early settlers to Benton County soon prevailed. A little over 20 years following the battle, Confederate and Union veterans held combined reunions at Pea Ridge.

A memorial to the Southern soldiers of the Confederacy proudly stands on the square in Bentonville. (Marilyn Collins.)

The face of early Arkansas was changing. In 1865, the Arkansas Immigration Aid Society organized to encourage white settlers from the North to come to the state, bringing their wealth with them. In 1869, the Arkansas River Valley Immigration Company helped bring Chinese laborers into the river valley. This was the same year that the transcontinental railroad was completed. Statewide census numbers recorded a population of 484,471 in 1870, almost doubling to 802,525 by 1880. Benton County also grew; its population in 1870 was 13,782 and, in 1880, 20,225.

Behind the scenes of the war's strife, the day-to-day life of residents in Northwest Arkansas continued but also changed. A thriving settlement was situated in the area before the establishment of Rogers in 1881, and people coming to the area soon found ways to prosper and help the community to grow. H.B. Horsley settled near Rogers and built the Electric Springs Hotel in 1867, and D.A. Oakley, who came to Benton County from Tennessee in 1868, established Oakley Chapel in 1869. The chapel's congregation met at Droke School until 1872, when the chapel was built. Oakley later became a leader in local industry. Prior to the Civil War, area children attended rural, one-room schools such as the War Eagle school, which was reportedly established in 1839. A complete system of public schools was not in place in Arkansas until 1868, and the first school building in Rogers was constructed in 1888. The change that was occurring throughout the county on many fronts would soon radically escalate with the introduction of the railroad into Benton County.

Two of the earliest settlers to the Rogers area were Robert and Elizabeth Sikes. Originally from Alabama, the Sikeses moved to Tennessee and then to Arkansas in 1854. When Robert Sikes died in 1856, he left 40 acres of land to each of his children, as was the custom. One of his sons, B.F. Sikes, returned to Tennessee in 1873 and married Tabitha Locke. But rumors soon reached him that the railroad was seeking a line through Arkansas. Sikes returned to Arkansas to purchase the inherited land of his siblings in order to make the consideration of the land more palatable to the railroad. Only one brother, J. Wade Sikes, retained his land south of where Cherry Street is located today.

B.F. Sikes then had 160 acres to entice the Frisco railroad to come through the Rogers area. Other local businessmen, including Henderson B. Horsley, Nathaniel S. Horsley, Major Simeon S. Horsley, William B. Horsley, George E. Wilson, Clark Brixey, Ben T. Oakley, and J.R. Swafford, also invested in bringing the railroad to Rogers. It was considered a philanthropic act for local businesspeople to invest in the railroad, as economic prosperity benefited everyone. Reduced costs for transporting goods to market increased farmers' profits, property values climbed, and business flourished with the influx of more people brought in by the railroad.

The St. Louis & San Francisco railroad, or the "Frisco" railroad as it was also called, was looking for a route to connect Missouri to Fort Smith, Arkansas. Since one owner with a large tract of land was easier to deal with than several owners with small individual acreage, Rogers had a strong chip to play in the selection process. Frisco's decision to run the line where it is today is owed in good part to the foresight and business acumen of B.F. Sikes.

History was already in the making and excitement in the air as the stage was set for the establishment of Rogers, a town that would play an important role in the early years of Benton County and the state. The stagecoach stopped here, telegraph lines were strung overhead, both Confederate and Union soldiers traversed the land, and, finally, the first citizens of Rogers enthusiastically greeted the railroad.

4. The Birth of Rogers

Power over the economic life or death of many towns in the early days of this country was often held by the railroad. An area selected as a railroad stop almost surely meant that a thriving town would emerge, and Rogers had all the right ingredients for success: abundant clean water, a temperate climate, fertile soil, ready means of transportation, and energetic, hard-working people. B.F. Sikes's accumulated block of land and the investment of other local businessmen, combined with the area's natural resources, put Rogers not only on the railroad line but made it a designated stop as well. In 1882, town residents donated an additional 20 acres to the railroad for a roundhouse. The railroad line in Benton County also helped to create the nearby towns of Lowell, Avoca, and Garfield.

On May 10, 1881, occurring almost simultaneously with the inaugural run of the Frisco on the newly laid tracks in Rogers, the town was named, businesses started, and a structure for governing established. Rogers gave the honor of its name to Captain Charles Warrington Rogers, the general manager of the St. Louis & San Francisco Railroad. Rogers and his wife, Mary Shaw Rogers, were proud of this distinction, and Captain Rogers even brought a group of businessmen from St. Louis to see his namesake city. Mrs. Rogers was actively interested in the town named for her husband and worked very hard for the betterment of its citizens. A member of the Congregational Church of St. Louis, Mrs. Rogers was instrumental in establishing the first church after Rogers was incorporated.

Number 17 was the first passenger train to come to Rogers, and the event brought out a crowd of curious spectators to see the noisy, fire-belching iron horse pull into town. Most people had never seen a train, and many traveled miles for this occasion, camping out overnight and bringing their own food. People were invited to tour the train, or they could ride it as far as the line was laid for 10¢ each.

Of course, there were dignitaries and speeches to mark this event. Judge James H. Berry welcomed the crowd, and T.E. Cassidy, the general freight agent from the railroad, gave the main address. According to accounts of the day, unfamiliarity with trains led to two amusing events. In a tie yard that adjoined the tracks, a group of young boys climbed the stacks of railroad ties to get a better look at this marvel. When the train stopped letting off steam, the boys thought the

Towns along the railroad tracks were often named for people associated with the train. Rogers was aptly named for Captain C.W. Rogers, the general manager and vice president of the St. Louis & San Francisco railroad. Rogers and his wife took an active part in the town during its early years. (Rogers Historical Museum.)

engine was about to blow up and ran for cover. In addition to this misunderstanding, at one time the train engineer got into the spirit of things and announced, "Look out, folks, I'm going to turn her around!" For a moment the crowd forgot that the train couldn't turn and scattered away to give her room. Life in Rogers was never the same!

The first depot in Rogers was located at First and Chestnut Streets but later moved to First and Cherry Streets. In future years, the incoming train would continue to be an event in Rogers. Santa Claus even arrived by train. Growing up, this author and her family would often go to the station on Sunday evenings after church to watch the train pull in. Her father loved the train and would tell tales from his boyhood days about "riding the rails," which took him from Rogers to as far away as California and Oregon. This author has since discovered that many families living in Rogers today remember when watching the train come in was a special event to be shared.

Rogers flourished and became one of the most progressive towns in Benton County. Rogers was incorporated on May 28, 1881, and soon after, the community elected its first mayor and city council from a voting population of about 600 people. J. Wade Sikes was elected mayor in June, along with J.W. Kimmons as recorder, Robert Sikes as marshal, and A.H. Oakley, John Dunagin, J.W. Stroud, J.W. Davis, and J.W. Hampton as members of the city council. The town founders and early families exemplified the character and intelligence that is still demonstrated by Rogers's citizens today. Business savvy, energetic leadership,

J. Wade Sikes, Benny Martin, and James Black were early leaders of the town and shared Civil War battlefield experiences at Pea Ridge. (Rogers Historical Museum.)

and foresight brought the railroad here, and upon this early vision the town was built. However, business growth was only part of the vision. The early citizens also initiated the development of churches, schools, public utilities, newspapers, city government, tourist attractions, and hotels.

Imagine living in a town before ordinances and regulations had been passed. These first actions taken by the Rogers city government reflect just how life was carried out in those early days, and most were directed either at the behavior of people or their animals within the city limits. City Ordinance No. 1, passed in 1882, exacted a fine from anyone slaughtering animals within the city limits except for their own family use, unless the animal was "rabid or furious, and is about to commit an injury to person or property or both." City Ordinance No. 3, passed in 1883, made it unlawful "to shoot firecrackers, skyrockets or torpedoes on the streets." City Ordinance No. 12, passed in 1891, forbid one to use "violent, profane or obscene language; sing indecent songs or cast stones, brick, brick-bat, or other mineral, metallic, wooden or vegetable substance at any building with the intent to inflict an injury upon the person . . . or drive any horse at an unusual speed along the streets." City Ordinance No. 18, passed in 1891, continued this line of reasoning, stating that citizens should "apply themselves to some honest calling or business" and not be found "loitering" around the "streets or bawdy houses or tippling houses, [or] be found in company with . . . lewd or lascivious persons." It was also frowned upon to spit on the streets or the floors of businesses. City Ordinance No. 22, passed in 1891, prohibited "the running at large of horses, mules or goats of any age, and bulls over the age of one year within the city limits." Another ordinance forbade "persons to fasten or hitch any horse, mule or other animal to any shade tree, fence or awning post." It was also disallowed to "bury dead animals" within the city limits.

Not all was peace and quiet in Rogers, and ruffians made life difficult for a time, intimidating local folks and extorting money to ensure that a person's property and body remained unharmed. Halloween pranks were sometimes more than pranks, and any wagon not locked up on that night was apt to disappear, reappearing elsewhere in town the next morning. The 1891 City Ordinance No. 23 made it unlawful for any person to wear or carry "any dirk or bowie-knife or sword or spear in a cane, brass or metal knucks [sic], razor or any pistol of any kind whatever as a weapon except such pistols as were used in the army or navy of the United States." The ordinance, however, did not apply to "persons on a journey" or law enforcement officers. Regulations regarding the misuse of the railroad by local kids included the 1894 City Ordinance No. 41 that prohibited "any minor to get on or swing to, any engine or car within the city limits unless he is an

This c. 1898 view from the corner of Elm and First Streets, looking north, shows a convivial crowd of pigs, horses, wagons, and townspeople catching up on the local news. (Rogers Historical Museum.)

employee of the railway company, or a passenger with the bona fide intent to ride to some other station."

Racial conflicts were not very evident in Rogers in the late nineteenth century though its citizens had been somewhat divided on the issue of slavery prior to the Civil War. Following the war, the population of African Americans, always stronger in the cotton counties, declined overall in Benton County. Rogers had no black population at this time, although several families resided in Bentonville. Minority men who worked laying the ties for the railroad in Rogers were not bothered by the townspeople; however, an African-American man caught alone might have been given a hard time by some of the rougher elements in town.

Health care conditions were primitive by today's standards of medicine, but several physicians were working in Rogers in the late 1800s and early 1900s. Doctors were often responsible for preparing and supplying their own medications until apothecary shops took on this task. A call in the middle of the night brought the doctor to a patient's home by wagon or carriage. Local doctors included Dr. Philo Alden, who was one of the county's first regular practicing physicians; Dr. William Curry, who served the community for over 70 years; Dr. Rufus Rice, who made the first house call by automobile; Dr. Rupert Cogswell, who is credited with building the first business on Walnut Street; Dr. W.H. Lennox and Dr. J.P. Brown, who erected a sanitarium on Third and Walnut Streets; and Dr. George M. Love, who operated a sanitarium on the site of the Butterfield Overland Stage stop at 506 East Spruce Street. Fortunately, many doctors' wives were also nurses and would accompany their husbands on calls.

Dr. Philo Alden was one of the first doctors in Benton County in the late 1800s. He not only helped the sick but also operated the Osage mill on Osage Creek. (Jerry Hiett.)

The first plat of 15 blocks of Rogers, registered in February 1881, was laid out by John B. Hely for "B.F. Sikes & S.T. Arkansas and Texas R.R. Co. of Arkansas and Mrs. Julia Allen proprietors." Dan W. German surveyed an additional 19 blocks of town, which was filed in August 1902. Both plats are shown in this 1902 record. (Maurice Kolman/City of Rogers.)

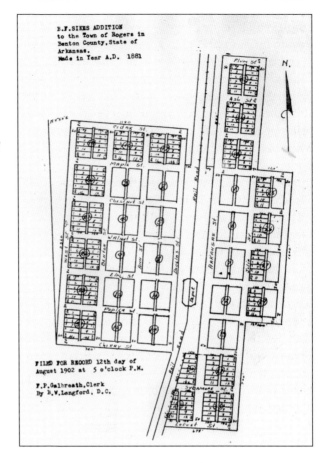

Being a doctor could be a dangerous business at times, especially when the procedure was painful and no anesthesia was available to sedate a thrashing or unruly patient.

B.F. Sikes was in charge of the post office in Cross Hollows prior to the organization of the town, and he brought the post office with him to Rogers. In those days, the post office moved to accommodate the new postmaster so it was usually not in one place very long. John A. Pertle, a local druggist, was appointed the first postmaster in Rogers. From 1881 to 1902, there were eight postmasters including J.H. Rackerby, D.W. Hinman (editor of the *Rogers Champion*), Campbell Stroud, D.A. Oakley, W.C. Chynoweth, John W. Puckett, and Leo K. Fesler.

Three major portions of the town streets were platted in 1881, and John P. Hely was hired by B.F. Sikes to lay out the first 15 blocks. Streets running from north to south were usually named for people, and streets running from east to west were named for trees. The first north-south streets were Julia, Arkansas, Douglas, Ann, and Benton (the latter three were renamed First, Second, and Third Streets in 1900). The first east-west streets were named Maple, Chestnut, Walnut, Elm, Poplar, and Cherry, and they maintain these designations today. Twelve lots were incorporated in each block. This configuration gave ownership of the five blocks between Arkansas Street and Douglas Street to the St. Louis, Arkansas & Texas Railroad. The first 180 lots were all sold by the end of the year.

Dan W. German drafted an additional 19 blocks for B.F. Sikes southwest of the original plat, and another 16 blocks were laid out that same year by J. Wade Sikes southwest of Cherry Street. The jog, most evident at Fourth and Cherry Streets, resulted from a disagreement between brothers B.F. and J. Wade Sikes on whether to place First, Second, Third, and Fourth Streets due north and south or parallel to the railroad tracks.

The next plat, which contained 45 blocks, was laid out to correspond with Electric Springs near what is now Lake Atalanta. Sanborn Insurance maps cover the next years of growth with maps dating 1896, 1901, 1908, 1914, and 1923.

How exciting it must have been in those early years to be part of the "firsts" of almost everything, to write on a clean slate. Imagine walking across streets that were more often than not muddy and made worse by the cattle, horses, chickens, goats, and hogs that, for a time, roamed freely. Long skirts were the fashion for women and even the cuffs of men's pants caught their share of the debris. The town took almost ten years to ban hogs and free-roaming animals from the streets. When sidewalks were finally built above the street level, it was a local joke that Rogers had built great sidewalks for the cows!

No office space existed, so buildings had to be constructed by enterprising individuals willing to take the risk. One story tells how, in 1881, John Cox, an

W.A. Miller Dry Goods Store opened in downtown Rogers in the early 1880s. The store is a good example of the frame, false-front store facades typical in those days. (Jerry Hiett.)

entrepreneur eager to set up shop before stores could be built, took advantage of a fallen oak tree near the railroad tracks. Taking the wheels off his wagon and setting it astride the branches, he opened up the first active business. Just six letters advertised his business, and, from the number of people who daily gathered round, his "saloon" was quite successful. Two other saloons, run by a Captain Blue and A. Greenstreet, soon opened.

Land adjacent to the railroad tracks became the center of commerce in Rogers. Dr. R.D. Cogswell is credited with erecting the first commercial building on Walnut Street, and W.A. Miller opened the first dry goods and general merchandise store. Early buildings were constructed mostly from wood but, after a fire in 1886 destroyed most of the downtown buildings, frame buildings were gradually replaced with brick construction.

Typical of early businessmen in Rogers were brothers J.E. and A.R. Applegate, who came to Rogers as young men looking for a business opportunity. They had only been in town ten days when they purchased the Pennington and McNeece Drugstore, located in a one-story building where Centennial Park is today. By the eleventh day of the brothers' residency, Applegate Drug store had come into being. Business was good and paralleled the town's own growth when J.E. bought out his brother's shares in 1882. As more space was needed, J.E. purchased a two-story building just down the street from his store's original location. In 1907, a new and larger drug store was built at 116 South First Street under the guidance and creative design of Mathews and Clark, an architectural firm out of St. Louis. Poor Richard's Gift and Confectionery is located there today.

Around the corner on Walnut Street is the Golden Rule building (part of a dime-store chain by that name), built around 1894 and having the distinction of housing the newspaper, the *Rogers Democrat*, for a time on the second floor. This paper preceded the *Rogers Daily News*. The Blue Goose Saloon was on the lower level for a few years. Several businesses have successfully come and gone in this building, including the offices of Dr. George M. Love (1905), Musselman's Bakery (1905), Leader Variety Store (1960), and Mode O' Day Dress Shop (1963), which now shares the space with Sue's (1998). The western portion of the building once was home to "Coin" Harvey (in the front room, 1902), Drs. Buckley and Lowery, the dentist Dr. Marshall (1925), Putman clothing, and Brewer's. In 1976, Tom & Jerry's Shoe Store occupied the first floor until Showcase Trophy and Gift Shop opened in 1999. "Golden Rule" is still painted on the building and is perhaps the oldest "sign" in downtown Rogers.

Many names are repeated over and over on business transactions, in company names, and on board of directors lists. These same leaders were also involved in churches, schools, and city government. *Goodspeed's 1889 History of Benton County, Arkansas* provides the following directory entry of the first businesses in Rogers:

> C.C. Davis, clothing; George Raupp, furniture; J.L. Merritt, restaurant;
> W.A. Miller, dry goods; Huffman and Wade, hotel; H.L. and S.T. Stokes,
> livery stable; Pratt and Gibbs and J.H. Rackerby, hardware; John Cox, A.

Greenstreet, Capt. Blue, saloons; Scroggins and Lowry, and Stokes and Bowman, groceries; Van Winkle and Blackburn, commission and wholesale lumber business; Huffman and Williams, McCubbins and Peck, produce and commission merchants; J.W. Brite, Berryhill and Durham, Mitchell and Dunagin, and J. Beasley, general merchandise.

W.E. Felker opened the first bank in Rogers, called appropriately the Bank of Rogers, in 1883, and his sons W.R. Felker and J.B. Felker served as bank officers. The Rogers Milling Company, the most extensive in Arkansas, was erected in 1886, and D. Wing & Brothers fruit evaporating and drying plant was the first established in Arkansas. But the main ingredient for the town's initial success was the community of people with business "know-how" who had arrived in Rogers even before commercial buildings were in place and the railroad rolled into town.

A list of industries and their owners does not even begin to tell the story of the impact of these businesses on employment and the bustling commerce. But business transactions in 1887, just six years after the founding of Rogers, were recorded in *Goodspeed's 1889 History of Benton County* as follows:

Four dry goods, clothing and notions, $60,000; seven groceries, $46,000; two hardware and implements, $23,000; three drugs and medicine, $15,000; one harness and saddlery, $2,000; one newspaper and job printing, $4,100; two butchers, $3,400; one variety store, $3,000; three millinery and ladies' furnishing, $4,000; one furniture and undertaking, $5,000; two hotels, $5,500; one barber, $1,500; one lumber, sash, doors, etc., $16,000; contracting and building, $28,000; produce, hides and furs, $45,000; grain and grain products, $123,300; live stock $44,500; 374 carloads ties, $18,000; 11,125 barrels apples shipped, $22,500; 15,000 bushels potatoes shipped, $6,000; evaporated fruit transactions, $60,000; miscellaneous, $20,000—total $565,600. Bank transactions and loans, $663,872. Grand total, $1,239,472.

Retail business was clearly thriving in Rogers, and soon, these legitimate merchants were protected by City Ordinance No. 10, approved in 1891, which required a license to do business. It was "unlawful for any person or persons to maintain, operate or carry any knife board, cane rack, striking machine, lifting machine, lung tester, swing, flying Dutchman, or any other device under whatever name it may be called for gain or lucre, on any street, alley or other public ground . . . without having first obtained a license." The cost of a license was to be no more than $25 and no less than $2.

Brothers H.L. and A.B. Stroud are early examples of successful local business people. Among other enterprises, H.L. was involved in the local grain elevator, Rogers Wholesale Grocery, the Bank of Rogers, and the Stroud Mercantile Company. In 1884, Stroud's Mercantile was located at First and Walnut Street, facing the railroad, but the business later moved to where the Felts Family Shoe

Stroud's Mercantile was a progressive store in downtown Rogers. Salesclerks, with comprehensive knowledge of their wares, stood ready to help their customers make the best selection. (Rogers Historical Museum/Betty Crum.)

Store is located today at 105 West Walnut Street and then to 114–116 West Walnut Street in 1898.

Keeping pace with his brother, A.B. Stroud joined the mercantile company at the age of 14 and, by age 17, took over the management of the store. A.B. Stroud introduced many new, perhaps radical, ideas for that time into store management. For instance, smoking was not allowed at Stroud's; the company paid their bills on the same day they were received; and price tags were placed on all merchandise, making the cost of goods the same for everyone. The traditional practice of shopping had forced customers to negotiate the price of an item with the clerk or storeowner, and the price could change according to who the customer was.

Hiring a woman as a salesclerk was also unheard of at that time, but Allie Inez Dodge soon became the first businesswoman in Rogers. Initially, she worked as a typesetter for the *Republican* newspaper, which was housed in the Mutual Aid Building, but she was later hired by Stroud's. This innovation in hiring proved so successful that Allie Dodge was soon followed by salesclerks Miss Edith Dunham, Miss Hallie Allumbaugh, Mrs. Hugh Rice, Mrs. Will Rogers, Mrs. Kelly Frost, Mrs. Will Minnick, a Mrs. Frazer, Mrs. F.S. Heffner, Mrs. Cora Van Winkle, and others.

Clerks were assigned a specific category of merchandise and were expected to be thoroughly knowledgeable in that area. If a man wanted to purchase a suit of

One of the first businesswomen in Rogers was Allie Inez Dodge. She worked first as a typesetter, then for Stroud's Mercantile as the first female salesclerk. Dodge was a graduate of the Rogers Academy. (Shirley and Dean Park.)

clothes ($10–$15), he saw Hal Hughes or Hugh Puckett, and Harvey Tuel was in charge of shoes ($2.75). A woman looking for lingerie or a dress ($1.98) was attended by Edith Dunham or one of the other female clerks. Mrs. Ida Woods was the millinery specialist, and a custom hat could be purchased for about 50¢. These 1898 prices look quite good to today's shoppers!

A.B. Stroud's management proved solid over the years. Even during the Depression, Stroud's was reported to be the only store that remained "in the black," and its name is still proudly displayed on this downtown building. In 1925, Stroud decided to look for a younger man to take over the management of the store, and he went to Birch Kirksey, the principal of Rogers High School, for advice. Kirksey recommended Harold Wardlaw, at the time a high school senior, and Stroud hired him. This selection proved a good one, as Wardlaw traveled to bigger cities to keep abreast of and study the latest fashions trends. Wardlaw and his silent partners, Lawrence, Gene, and Ray Harris, purchased Stroud's in 1949. They later sold the business, and Wardlaw repurchased it, with H.K. Scott and Bill Crum as his partners, in 1964. Stroud's finally closed its doors in 1993 after 109 years in business.

Many of the handsome, brick buildings that housed Rogers's early businesses have weathered the decades since the late 1800s, including the Union Block Building (1897) on the southeast corner of Walnut and Second Street, Burnham

Block Building (1896) on the northwest corner of Elm and First Streets where Vinson Square is now, the Opera Block (1896) at 104–106 West Walnut Street, the Juhre Block (1894) at 202–204 West Walnut, and the Bank of Rogers building (1905–1907) at 114 First Street. In the early days, many downtown stores stayed open in the evening, and owners often swept their own sidewalks or spent time polishing the brass appointments on their display cases. Hitching posts were conveniently placed beside the sidewalks so customers did not have to walk through the mud from their wagons or carriages or encounter livestock wandering at will on the unpaved streets. A healthy competition also existed among these merchants, a competition that was even played out in a baseball game in the late 1800s that pitted the First Street merchants against the Walnut Street merchants.

Downtown Rogers was not just about business but also included room for entertainment and the arts. W.A. Miller owned and managed the Opera House located on the second floor of 104–106 West Walnut Street. Many communities boasted an opera house, but not so many actually ever witnessed an opera. In Rogers, the voices still echo from the illustrious speakers and performers who entertained local crowds. Thomas Edison's invention, the vitascope, was on display in 1896. In addition to hosting events of national or statewide significance, the Opera House also provided a place for the local folks to dance on Friday nights, hold banquets, or stage political discourses. A third floor was added in 1903 to add more seating, and the building was again remodeled in 1918 to relocate the stage and add even more seating. The Opera House flourished as a center for entertainment until the movies—a new and novel source of

Entertainment was readily available at the downtown Opera House, pictured here c. 1895, on the corner of First and Walnut Streets. (Rogers Historical Museum.)

Still a notable landmark in downtown Rogers, the Juhre building has been home to a variety of businesses, including a meat market, drug store, and home decorating shop. (Opal Beck.)

entertainment—began to draw crowds. Ironically, the first motion picture in Rogers was shown at the Opera House in 1897. The lower level of this building has been home to the Rexall Drug Store (1898), Benton County Realty Company (1911), and L.A. Coleman Shoe Company (1918), and is currently the home of Dixieland Shoes (1981).

Another landmark building in Rogers is the Juhre Block (1894) at 202–204 West Walnut. It housed the Rogers Grocery Company prior to 1900, at which time Charles Juhre purchased the building and opened a meat market, sharing space with J.W. Ford Grocery and Feed Store downstairs and the offices of Dr. J.G. Robison upstairs. It is currently home to Prized Possessions, an upscale gift and decorating shop. Fortunately, the architectural features of many downtown buildings from these early years have been preserved today. (Brochures and booklets available at the Rogers Historical Museum serve as guides to architecturally significant residential and commercial buildings in Rogers.)

Fresh spring water was in abundance in the Rogers area and was one of the major attractions for early settlers and, later, the railroad. Diamond Springs, which got its name from the sparkling bubbles effervescing in its water, was the source of Rogers's water supply. J.A.C. Blackburn, W.K. Dyer, and B.F. Dyer organized a public water system in 1888, and a brick structure served as the first water tower. Other springs in the area included Callahan Springs, Esculapia Spring (later named Electric Springs), Silver Spring, Osage Spring, Frisco Spring (later called Pump Springs for its role with the railroad), Pruitt Springs, and Cave Springs.

Popular belief held that some spring waters had healing properties. For instance, Electric Springs was so named because people thought its "electricity" was curative; supposedly, a metal object held in the water would become magnetized. A hotel and sanitarium were even built at Electric Springs to take advantage of the healthful effects of the water, but all that now remains are the spring waters at the side of Highway 12. The healing waters of springs were reported at one time or another to cure ailments including neuralgia, rheumatism, scrofula (sores), dropsy, and dyspepsia. According to J. Dickson Black's report in *Benton County Back Then*, a man named "James Bevel was cured of scrofula of ten years standing, which had baffled the skill of many physicians. Both his body and limbs were matted with sores and deep ulcers, and the bone in one leg burst and came out in small particles. He had not walked for three years and most of the time was not able to raise his head from his pillow. After using the water six weeks he could sit up, and now after using it four months, is out walking over the mountains hunting game."

In the mid-nineteenth century, early settlers and people drawn to the Rogers area by its waters found few public accommodations available. Sometimes local homes were open to guests, but more often, people had to make do by seeking

Resorts were popular in and around Rogers. The Lane Hotel, built in 1928–1929 for both businessmen and tourists, was convenient to the railroad. (Rogers Historical Museum.)

shelter for the night in the surrounding woods or be lucky enough to own a tent. But it was not long before investors began to build hotels to capture this market, though the smaller establishments soon went out of business. The corner of First and Poplar (where the *Rogers Daily News* was later located and now the site of Castor's Muffler & Alignment) was once the site of three historic hotels: the Jones Hotel (1897), the Nashburg Hotel (1906), and Hotel Main (1910). Traveler's Hotel (1904), located at Third and Walnut Streets, was one of the longest continually operated hotels in Rogers. The Commercial Hotel (1885) was situated at First and Elm Streets. Later in 1929, the Lane Hotel would open on Popular Street. These hotels, plus smaller boarding houses and the various resort accommodations in Monte Ne, would continue to draw visitors to the waters and to this beautiful part of the Ozark Mountains for years to come.

Perhaps not surprisingly, hotel owners actively looked at passengers on the trains that came through Rogers as likely customers. Not missing a trick, city officials passed City Ordinance No. 47, which stated that "all Hotel boarding houses and restaurant keepers in the City of Rogers, Arkansas, who in person or by porter or agent shall meet the trains in said City and solicit customers guests or boarders shall pay to the said City of Rogers a license fee in the sum of $12.00 per annum."

Available water also made it possible for the town to have a functioning fire department. In 1888, Rogers Hose Company No. 1 was organized with 18 charter members and John H. Rebholtz as fire chief. A hand-pulled, two-wheel hose cart was used until 1915, when the first motorized vehicle was purchased. When a fire broke out, the men would pull out the cart and race to the fire. City Ordinance No. 58, approved in 1907, stated that "a fee of $2.50 will be given hereafter by the City of Rogers, to the person owning a two-horse vehicle who shall arrive first at the front of the City Hall with his vehicle in response to a fire alarm and who either in person or by his employee shall convey the hose cart with speed to the place where the fire maybe [*sic*] and return the same back to the front of the City Hall after the fire is extinguished as shall be directed by the Captain of the fire company."

Electricity was first brought to downtown Rogers in 1895, but it was not offered as a full-time service. Lights were only supplied from 8 p.m. to 10 p.m. This service proved more costly than the city could handle and was eventually discontinued, except on First Street. This decision by the city was not a popular one in the wider community, but electrical service could be purchased for a fee. Electrical service was improved and expanded in 1905, when a new light plant began operation; however, as if adding insult to injury, when service was reconnected in 1905, the stronger current blew out most of the light bulbs in town! The city continued in financial difficulty and in 1898 took further action to conserve the city treasury. Working with an annual budget of only $1,200, the city was barely able to pay its water bill. Desperate measures were called for and a source of money was found to pay this bill by reducing the city marshal's salary by $15 a month.

Pictured here c. 1889, the men of Rogers Hose Company No. 1 are ready to combat fire in downtown Rogers equipped with only a hand-pulled hose cart. (Rogers Fire Department.)

In 1897, Judge Milard Berry of Springdale connected Rogers to his telephone system and set up an office that was first located in the dry goods store at 104 West Walnut Street. But this service was initially unsatisfactory. The system was crude and consisted of iron wires strung on the crossbars of poles made from local trees. These wires soon rusted in the weather and resulted in much "scratchy" conversation. In 1899, Rogers's original six-line system was replaced with a 25-line switchboard. Calls were placed directly with the operator. Ida Smith served as the first telephone operator in Rogers. Stella Clarke and Anna Murdock also became operators in Rogers, and W.C. Davis (the troubleshooter), Frank Dunn, and Ed Johnson rounded out the telephone's early employees. The Rogers system became part of the Northwest Arkansas Telephone Company, which was organized in 1900. In 1910, the company sold out to the Southern Telephone Company, which in turn was bought by Southwestern Bell in 1911. City Ordinance No. 54 set the telephone cost for a private residence at not in excess of $1.50 per month and not in excess of $2 per month for business houses or offices.

Religion was an important part of Rogers from the arrival of its earliest settlers. Several churches were organized even before the incorporation of the town, including Pleasant Hill Baptist Church (established in 1852) and New Hope Church (1858). More churches were organized in Rogers after its official 1881 founding, and the community's rather rapid growth soon required added space and new buildings for the purpose of worship. Before permanent churches were built, religion was often delivered on horseback or, in some cases, by foot. One such missionary was Reverend G.C. Harris, who traveled through the Ozarks preaching and establishing churches. According to his son Elmer Harris, Reverend Harris would "walk his circuit wearing the tall black hat of the 1870s–80s period, but with his shoes tied by their strings swinging around his neck—so they wouldn't wear out." Just before arriving at his preaching station, he would put on his shoes, which he saved for the "important purpose of preaching 'the power of God unto salvation to them that believe.' " He, along with Reverend Jasper Dunagin and Reverend W.W. Harris, organized the First Baptist Church in Rogers in 1883 with five charter members: Mrs. C.D. Rearick, Miss Lula Rearick, Mrs. Alice King, Mrs. Pagett, and A.D. Leggett. Reverend Dunagin became their first pastor. First Baptist Church's first building was constructed in 1885 on Second and Cherry Streets, and their second building was erected on the same site in 1905.

In January 1967, Erwin Funk, editor of the *Rogers Democrat*, shared a story of what life was like for these early preachers with the publication of an article written by Reverend G.C. Harris in the *Benton County Pioneer*. It seems that after a harrowing ride on a runaway stage, Reverend Harris arrived in Rogers and met Reverend Wade Sikes, the mayor of the town. "He and I were going to the Electric

LEFT: *The original building of the First Baptist Church, on the corner of Second and Cherry Streets, was dedicated in 1887. A larger, brick sanctuary was constructed in 1905 on this site but later burned. (Rogers Historical Museum.)*

RIGHT: *Reverend George Crittenden Harris, standing beside his "bee-gum" hat, was a circuit rider throughout the Ozarks. He was instrumental in organizing the First Baptist Church in Rogers. (Shirley Park.)*

Mrs. C.W. Rogers helped provide the means to build and furnish the Congregational Church on land donated by B.F. Sikes. The church, built in 1881, stood where the Mutual Aid Union building was later constructed at the northwest corner of Second and Poplar Streets. (Rogers Historical Museum.)

Springs. There was a saloon under a tent in the east part of town. Someone threw a rock at my hat and hit Uncle Wade. I held the reins while he got out and made for the saloon. There were thick bushes back of the tent and as Bro. Sikes entered the front door, the gang ran out of the back door and hid in the underbrush." Harris's misadventures with his "bee-gum" hat continued when a young boy, fascinated by his hat during a church service at Cave Springs, tried to sit in it, bringing a stop the service. But, finally, the infamous hat was passed along, as Harris recounts, "My next place of any importance was in the Indian Territory. I stopped the first night at an Indian hut and a small Indian boy got frightened at my plug hat (which by this time was looking rather dilapidated) and so I finally gave the old hat to a Negro preacher who admired it." Another unusual incident in the life of this traveling minister occurred when Reverend Harris was falsely accused of robbing a bank in Springdale. "I asked them if there was not going to be preaching at the schoolhouse. They said yes, and I said I was going to do the preaching, so they decided to arrest me after the preaching. Then they decided to let me go."

The strong religious faith of the early founders of Rogers is evident in the generosity of local leaders, who often deeded the land for church buildings or were instrumental in funding the local churches. Many early congregations first met in schoolhouses or in the homes of members. The Congregational Church was the first church organized in Rogers after the town incorporated. This church was sponsored by Mrs. C.W. Rogers and built on land donated by B.F. Sikes in 1881. Mrs. Rogers, a member of the Congregational Church in St. Louis, called

The Oakley Chapel congregation first met in Droke School until a permanent sanctuary was built in 1896. Members came to church on Sunday morning to the sound of bells ringing in the tower overhead. (Rogers Historical Museum.)

upon her home church to donate the pulpit and pews, and the railroad brought the furnishings and building materials to town at no cost. Mrs. Rogers was also instrumental in getting the church built on the corner of Second and Poplar Streets where the Mutual Aid Union building now stands. At that time, the church was placed amid stumps and trees and was bordered by a muddy street on each side. Reverend R.P. West was the church's first pastor. The Congregational Church merged with the First Presbyterian Church at Fourth and Walnut Streets in 1911, and that building was later moved to Fourth and Olive to become the new Catholic church. A new Presbyterian church, designed by A.O. Clarke, was built in 1914. This structure was torn down and a new church built at South Twenty-sixth Street in 1994.

Organized in 1869 in the old Droke schoolhouse, Oakley Chapel United Methodist Church constructed its first permanent home in 1896 on land donated by Haywood and Elizabeth Oakley in 1872. The first trustees were W.J. Oakley, Haywood Oakley, G.W. Droke, S.H. Shelton, and Elsby Oakley. The first Sunday school superintendent was Jim Oakley, and Audra McFarlin Rakes was the congregation's pianist for over 65 years. The First Christian Church was organized in Rogers in 1886 and held its first service in a new building at Third and Poplar Streets in 1890. The congregation, including B.A. Riggs, Mrs. W.H. Fowler, Mr. and Mrs. H.L. Stroud, Mr. and Mrs. J.D. Hensley, Mrs. Minnick, and Captain Benton, pledged themselves "to love one another, to work together in harmony, and to build up the cause of the Master in our town and vicinity."

The Methodist Episcopal Church, South, and the First Methodist Episcopal Church, North, were two early churches that organized in 1883 and were consolidated in 1937. Each congregation moved several times before coming together in the same building designed by A.O. Clarke on Third and Elm Streets (built in 1908). In 1968, the joint church became known as the Central United Methodist Church, but the congregations became separate entities once again in 1994–1995. Today, the First United Methodist Church remains at Third and Elm Streets, and the newly constructed church at New Hope Road and Twenty-sixth Streets is now the Central United Methodist Church.

Other churches soon followed, and suffice it to say, churches that organized in Rogers and the surrounding community reflected the values of people in the area. Many church leaders were also civic leaders and played active roles in the affairs of the town.

Many faith-based organizations were also present in early Rogers, including such groups as the Salvation Army, the Women's Christian Temperance Union (WCTU), and the Anti-Saloon League. The WCTU and other like-minded groups were very successful in ridding the town of alcohol. An ordinance passed in 1905 made it a violation to sell liquor in Benton County. The WCTU also took on the evils of smoking and was supported by several Rogers merchants who quit selling the "makin's." John E. Brown Sr., who joined the Salvation Army in Rogers in 1897, went on to found John Brown University in Siloam Springs.

Education was also a major priority in the early development of Rogers, as Mrs. C.W. Rogers believed that education and religion worked hand in hand. Following a failed attempt by local business people to build a school, Mrs. Rogers garnered support from her husband and members of the Congregational Church in St. Louis and set about attending to the educational needs of this fledgling town. Townspeople were not inclined to pay higher taxes to cover the cost of public education, favoring instead private school leadership. After several public meetings, the town agreed to furnish a school site and half the building costs. The Congregational Church adopted Rogers as a mission and covered the shortfall between the tuition receipts and the faculty salaries. They also agreed to help finance the construction costs. Over the years, the school buildings were improved and modified as funds for these efforts waned and flowed. The land selected for the school was owned by J. Wesley Stroud and is the land on which Tillery School now stands. At the time, the property was covered with thick brush and trees and was known as a great spot for deer hunting.

Ten men, who represented either the businessmen in town or the Congregational Church, served as the first trustees of the newly formed Rogers Academy, which opened in 1883. They were W.A. Miller, George Raupp, J.W. Frey, Dr. J.C. Pennington, Joshua Huffman, W.R. Felker, Reverend R.T. Marlow, J.W. Barnett, Dr. J.C. Freeland, and J. Wesley Stroud.

Academically, the new school was an outstanding example in Arkansas. It surpassed other secondary schools, ranking higher than the high schools of Fort Smith, Pine Bluff, and Little Rock, and many graduates of Rogers Academy went on to earn higher education degrees and pursue professional careers. Language courses were offered in Latin, German, French, and Greek; higher mathematics classes in geometry and trigonometry; science courses in zoology, physiology, botany, chemistry, and physics; as well as classes in ancient and modern history, debating, elocution, and economics. Religion was also part of the curriculum, and each student was required to attend at least one Sunday service. Classes in music—including music theory and instruction in organ, violin, cello, guitar, clarinet, flute, piano, and other instruments—were offered as funds allowed, and the school orchestra and choir were known to provide entertainment for the students as well as the wider community. Students also had the opportunity to present essays, hold poetry readings, and conduct debates sponsored by the Literary Society.

Although the school library was not extensive by today's standards, many current magazines and 2,000 books were available for use by students. They could study in the library and use the material at no cost; however, it cost 25¢ to check out a book.

Erwin Funk's research on the history of the Rogers Academy, presented in the *Rogers Daily News* in 1936, gave great insight into day-to-day life at the school. The Academy adhered to a firm code of ethical behavior. According to an early catalog, "Superfluous gallantry will not be allowed," which meant that a boy could only go out with any one girl three times within a school year. Upon request by her parents, a female student could be denied any boyfriend at all while in school. No

The Rogers Academy offered the opportunity of education to the children of the town, and its students participated in a highly academic curriculum and fledgling sports program. This view shows the east facade of the school. (Rogers Historical Museum.)

form of tobacco was allowed and students who displayed "stuck-up, rude, or ill-mannered behavior" were not welcome. The school was also a "closed campus," which meant that students were not allowed off the grounds without permission. In addition to academic achievement, the school emphasized teaching students to be courteous and kind. According to remarks made by students, the school was a wonderful and welcoming place to be. There seems to be no record of any student being expelled, so the atmosphere, although strict, did not seem to be harsh.

In spite of the rules regarding courtship, several students did later marry. Among those were Urie Harris to Mattie Dickson (both Class of 1898); John Simon Sager (Class of 1889) to Allie Dodge (Class of 1892); and Albin Brixey (Class of 1892) to Ethel Buchanan (Class of 1895).

In 1892, tuition at Rogers Academy was about $94, a price that included room, board, and books. Music courses were an additional fee. For those students rooming at Elizabeth Hall, which was built in 1892 to accommodate out-of-town students, board amounted to $1.50 per week. Except for a stove and a lamp, which were provided, students had to furnish their own rooms. Students often bartered their skills in carpentry or painting for tuition, and students from neighboring farms sometimes bartered food, a practice which also ensured that students never left the table hungry.

Needless to say, the Academy was successful because of the efforts of the local people who served on the board of trustees, the school's donors, its well-educated faculty, committed parents, and students who adapted well to the stimulating academic environment. Other early members of the school's board of trustees include John C. Flenniken, Captain J.B. Steele, W.K. Dryer, G.S. Ricker, A.J. Smith, Senator J.A.C. Blackburn, Thomas Douglas, G.W. Rich, J.S. Garretson, John Hovey Dodge, S.B. Wing, H.A. Oakley, David Wing, Clark Brixey, Reverend J.G. Bailey, Reverend R.C. Walton, John W. Stroud, E.M. Funk, and James H. Berry (governor of Arkansas in 1881 and senator from Arkansas in 1885). It was not unusual for a trustee to serve for several years in their leadership capacity.

Professor J.W. Scroggs headed the school as principal for the first 15 years of its existence, and he was succeeded by Reverend Morrison Weimer in 1898. The school graduated 27 classes from its first in 1887 to its last in 1913, including 129 female graduates and 106 male graduates.

In her valedictory address entitled "Open Sesame" on June 8, 1892, 19-year-old Allie Inez Dodge summed up the overall direction of the teaching at the Academy in words that might still be relevant to today's graduating seniors. She listed the skills of capacity, preparation, earnestness, intelligence, and religious belief as keys to open the door of future success.

> With capacity a man's work becomes a luxury. There is a freshness, a vivacity, a real harmony in it out of which he gets music. His work is to his soul what the soft evening wind is to the strings of an aeolian harp— his life is a psalm, and every day is lighted up with the inspiration of success . . . . A person may have ever so good an opening but if he has

not made the necessary preparation which would fit him to fill that position, or in other words if he has not the right key, he will not be able to unlock the door and must leave it for a more fortunate one who has secured this key. Thus every door is closed to those who in the morning of life have not made the necessary preparation which would have fitted them to fill these places, and others step in and fill the places they might have had. Make a thorough preparation for life for we know not what positions of responsibility and trust may be offered to us.

. . . Is it not so, that in order to succeed we must be useful to others. Make our selves felt in the world, make the world better for our having lived in it. Then it is we have made our life a success and not till then.

O my class mates, we stand today before the closed doors of the future. We know not what opening awaits us. Let us make a thorough preparation for life and leave the rest with God.

Not all of the emphasis at Rogers Academy, however, was placed on academics and musical performances. A rough and rugged football team set records, if not always in winning scores, with the physical courage they displayed by playing in conditions unheard of today. In an article in the *Rogers Daily News*, Erwin Funk relates that in 1900 William A. Draggett coached a team made up of Academy students but not officially sanctioned by the school due to opposition to the game. The first game fielded a team of 11 players, 7 of whom had never seen a football game before and only 1 or 2 of whom had ever played! One novice player just grabbed every leg he could find on the opposition and held on. The story goes that after every play, his team had to pry him off his tackle. Not surprisingly, Rogers lost that game 27 to 0. The players on this first team were Joe Cowan, Blaine Crow, Will Wardlaw, Commodore Roller, Ezra Snavely, Oliver McGinnis, Orville Campbell, Emmett Huffman, Solon Milton, Finis Miller, and W.A. Draggett, with Mack Rodgers, James Keith, L.H. Edgerton, Erwin Juhre, and Elmer Wilson as substitutes.

Two years later, this green team won the championship. According to Erwin Funk's description of these early games in the *Rogers Daily News* some years later, "Bentonville, Springdale, and Fayetteville refused to play Rogers that year admitting they were too badly outclassed." The team's adventures included a story of one player, Emmett Huffman, who, after breaking his arm in a game, got a piece of tin to cover his cast and played anyhow—much to the consternation of the opposing team. Ed Richards played with a broken collarbone, and Finis Miller ended up on the sidelines with two members of the opposing teams sitting on him to keep him out of the game. Football was banned and reinstated several times over the next few years, as the safety of the players became a concern.

Girls' basketball at Rogers Academy began in 1900 under the coaching of Miss Jessie Hayes, and the first players were Zuleki Blake, Sadie Boley, Hattie Chapin, Lucile Carse, Georgia Dyer, Edith Dunham, Mabel Juhre, Gertrude Dickson, and Celina Beaulieu.

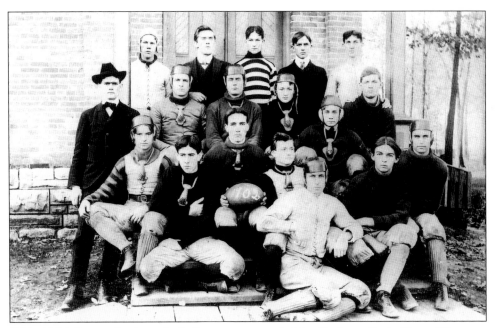

This 1902 Rogers Academy football team was coached by Professor Paul Albert. The team won its first and only championship game. (Rogers Historical Museum.)

Whether in academics or sports, business or politics, the names of Rogers Academy graduates often appear later in Rogers's history as community leaders. The Academy, which began with just 2 students in its first graduating class in 1887 (W.H. Allred and J.H. Barr), grew to 22 graduates in 1896 and ended with 8 graduates in 1913. In 1914, an agreement was made with the Rogers School District to transfer the property to the public schools. The Academy's indebtedness was covered by the Congregational Church Educational Society at a cost of $9,000, and school bonds that amounted to $12,000 covered the rest. According to the Academy's brochure, "There is but one childhood and but one chance for education. Get the best; that will be none too good."

Another learning opportunity for the people of Rogers was the Chautauqua, a national educational enrichment program sponsored by Sunday school teachers in Chautauqua, New York. Many citizens of Rogers attended local lectures, musical programs, and other entertainments presented by this group, and these programs remained popular until the 1920s, when they were eclipsed by radio and motion pictures.

In the late 1800s and early 1900s, numerous civic and fraternal organizations for men were prominent, though many faded in importance as other activities began to draw more interest. The International Order of Odd Fellows was established in 1883; the first Masonic Lodge in 1887; the Knights of Pythias in 1890; the Young Men's Christian Association in 1907; and the Elks Lodge in 1911. Other organizations of the period included the Woodmen of the World, the Ancient

F.A. Mason, the editor of the New Era *newspaper in the 1880s, provided an excellent glimpse of early Rogers in letters to his wife, highlighting sketches of town life. (Rogers Historical Museum.)*

Order of United Workmen, and the Moose Lodge, and the first scouting troop for boys in Rogers was organized in 1911. The Elks Lodge met in the building situated on the corner of Walnut and Second Street, and the current owner of that structure, the Benchmark Group, has recently restored the Elks sign to the front facade of the building.

Various newspapers, which sprang up almost simultaneously with the incorporation of the town, faithfully recorded the happenings in Rogers, though the newspapers themselves changed owners, locations, and editors on a fairly regular basis, and the records of these changes sometimes differ. There were at least 13 newspapers operating under separate mastheads in Bentonville and 9 in Rogers during the late 1800s.

The first newspaper in Rogers, the *Rogers Champion* owned by D.W. Hinman, debuted on September 1, 1881, about four months after the arrival of the railroad in Rogers. A quirk in the postal system often paired the job of local postmaster with the job of local newspaper editor—based on that editor's support of the winning political candidate for president. This could make the postmaster either very popular in his local community, or not. Hinman was a Republican and as Grover Cleveland was the Republican President at the time, Hinman also became the postmaster in Rogers.

Some businessmen in Rogers who were staunch Democrats chose to take their mail directly to the train for deposit rather than going through the post office as a way of expressing their distaste for Hinman's political preferences. Since the salary of the postmaster was directly tied to the amount of mail he handled, the effect on Hinman must have been serious because his newspaper folded in record time. This action was even more significant for J.H. Rackerby, who had been replaced by Hinman as postmaster. Rackerby went to work for the Frisco railroad to handle the mail posted on the train, and it was, in a way, sweet revenge when townspeople brought their mail to him in his new capacity as the mail clerk on the train rather than taking their mail to his replacement in the downtown post office. Rackerby was later credited as being the "oldest railway mail clerk west of the Mississippi" in both age and in years of service. The post office moved with the times and wherever the next "politically correct" editor had established his office, that is where the post office was also located.

Following the Civil War, Republican "carpetbaggers" who traveled to the South in order to take advantage of the depressed post-war conditions were not very welcome in the region. Despite this general hostility, a visitor to Rogers from Indiana wrote in a letter, published by the *Champion*, that he was surprised Republicans were not lynched on sight. "I find that Republicans have as many rights here as the Democrats and need have no fear of being molested." Signing the letter only "W.H.T.," the author also expressed his feelings about Rogers, saying, "Your citizens are sociable, enterprizing [*sic*] and full of vim. A good country surrounds you and my opinion is that your chance of becoming a city of cosmopolitan proportions are very flattering."

About ten days after the *Rogers Champion* was founded, the *Rogers New Era* was organized with James A. Graham and his stepson F.A. Mason as the newspaper's owners/editors. Letters from F.A. Mason to his wife, Hattie, provide considerable insight into the struggles of getting a newspaper up and running and the competitive spirit that existed in the news business in Rogers. One major concern for Mason was getting a printing press to Rogers. "We are here waiting for our Press and material. It has not come yet. Do not know what is the matter. Hope it will be in to-night." Mason's comment on the other newspaper in town is also telling: "There is a fellow here with an office. He is a Republican and will not accomplish anything. . . . There are some radicals here who will support the other paper but I do not think it will live more than six months." His prediction proved to be true.

Mason also recorded some interesting figures related to the cost of living in Rogers. In 1881, housing was hard to come by and many people were living in tents or sheds. The cost of a room was $10 per month, and building a two-room house could be done for about $150. It cost $13 for a ticket on the railroad from St. Louis to Rogers. Other prices mentioned by Mason included the following: "Bacon was 12 1/2 cents, six to seven pounds of coffee cost around one dollar . . . a nice rocking chair for $1.50 . . . and other chairs from $4 to $6 per set." Mason had high hopes for Rogers and painted the community as quite promising in his letters home.

> There is a great deal of business being done here. This is bound to be the largest town in North Arkansas and it will not be long about it. . . .The people here are nearly all strangers one to the other. I attended church last evening, the Episcopalean [sic]. They have a beautiful church house nicely finished inside, but their minister cannot preach much. . . . The people here seem clever and sociable [sic] and I think this will be a pleasant enough place to live after the people get settled down and houses built.

Next on the publishing scene was the *Rogers Republican*, which was established in 1888 and owned by L.C. Warner and C.F. Honeywell. A group of Rogers businessmen decided that bringing new homeowners to Rogers from the North might be a good idea after all, and they helped to finance the Republican newspaper as a means of attracting this particular group.

In 1890, the *New Era* was published by Smythe and J.W. McCammon, who later changed the name of the newspaper to the *Rogers Democrat*. H.M. Butler then purchased the paper in 1892. To this weekly paper was soon added the first daily paper, the *Rogers Daily Democrat,* in 1894. This newspaper, located above a hardware store between Walnut and Elm on First Street (now the site of a parking lot next to Poor Richard's Gift and Confectionery), was only published as a daily for a few months. In 1896, E.M. Funk and his son Erwin next bought the *Democrat,* and in 1919, Erwin took over control of the newspaper, although his father continued to participate. In his memoirs, entitled *64 Years in Newspapering in Arkansas, 1896–1960*, Erwin Funk expressed the following sentiments:

> Perhaps the greatest satisfaction I have received from my newspaper work has been the number of people who show or tell me of obituaries, now ragged and worn with age and re-reading, clipped and treasured. Many are kept in the family Bible. A year or two ago at a Rotary luncheon I sat with an elderly man from California who was surprised and pleased to learn that I had written of the death of a niece in Springdale in 1896. (By the way, it was the first I had written in Arkansas.) He said it was a treasured heirloom and he thought the best he had ever read. I must admit it was over-written but it had a personal touch that had won the hearts of the relatives. . . . In the files were letters from all over the country thanking me for that last tribute to loved ones. A five or six line item about a physician who was at the point of death, saying he was 'one of the best loved men in our community' brought me word from his wife that it gave him more real pleasure than would a wagon-load of flowers. Every editor must make his own decisions on such matters but to me every issue of the *Democrat* was a personal letter to my readers.

The first linotype (c. 1919) in Rogers was operated by Stella Clark for the Democrat. *(Rogers Historical Museum.)*

Funk and his father were both experienced in the newspaper business; they already owned the *Springdale Democrat* at the time they bought the newspaper in Rogers. Upon selling the paper to Funk, H.M. Butler added to his compliments of Funk's abilities and integrity by giving some good advice to the town that remains relevant today:

> A good newspaper is the best advertising matter a town can send out and whenever the business men of a town neglect their home papers they are crippling their best interests and inviting enterprise and capital to remain outside. The local newspaper is the phonograph of the town and community and gives to the world the impressions it receives from the business and professional men. It is very important that every one should understand the necessity of giving the local papers a generous and hearty support.

Other newspapers came and went during the latter part of the 1800s, and the Arkansas Newspaper Project listed the following newspapers in Rogers during this period: *Rogers Champion* (first published in 1881), *Rogers New Era* (1881), *Rogers Republican* (1888), *Methodist Herald* (1889), *Democratic Sentinel* (1890), *Enterprise* (1891), *Rogers Leader* (1896), *Rogers Enterprise* (1897), and *Cain's Thomas Cat.* (1897).

The *Rogers Daily Post* was first published in 1910 by John W. Nance and Ernest W. Vinson. After several changes in ownership, the paper was renamed the *Northwest Arkansas Times*. James P. Shofner, another new owner, changed the name to *Rogers Daily News* in 1927. This paper and the *Rogers Democrat* came under one

Tom Morgan was a well-known figure about town. He wrote for national magazines and the Kansas City Star, in *addition to running a Rogers newsstand. (Rogers Historical Museum.)*

masthead, *The Rogers Daily News*, in 1937. The Donrey Media Group, the current owner, purchased the paper in 1955 and renamed it the *Northwest Arkansas Morning News*, now shortened to *The Morning News*.

Cost was an important factor in the demise of many newspapers. Equipment and materials had to be brought in by rail, and qualified local labor was not easy to find. Libel laws had to be studied carefully to avoid successful suits from disgruntled readers. Erwin Funk was once quoted in an Oklahoma City paper on the dangers of being an editor: "Horsewhipping had gone out of vogue by the time I became an editor but once in awhile a man would announce that he was going to whip the man who 'wrote him up'. When that happened, Father was always the editor at fault and I took a leave of absence from the office." In addition to these difficulties, the mechanics of the newspaper business could also be dangerous. More than one editor in Rogers lost part of a hand while operating the press, an accident that became almost a rite of passage for the true newspaperman.

Joining this stimulating environment of writers and publishers in 1890 was Tom Morgan, a nationally known writer and humorist who moved from Kansas to Rogers. Morgan wrote for many national publications at the time, including *Ladies' Home Journal*, *Life*, and the *Saturday Evening Post*; he was also a short-story contributor to the *Kansas City Star*. In 1893, Morgan opened a store in Rogers that sold cigars, schoolbooks, periodicals, and a large selection of postcards.

As they entered the twentieth century, the citizens of Rogers did not wait around for "what's coming next," but they made it happen.

5. POLITICAL AND SOCIAL CHANGE

Rogers was not immune to the dramatic social changes that swept through the country during the early 1900s, as war, no longer localized, encompassed much of the world. Benton County men had fought on neighboring soil during the war with Mexico and on their own land during the Civil War. Now, with the beginning of World War I, many men traveled far away from home for the first time and experienced different cultures, as well as sometimes life-shattering experiences, overseas.

The United States entered World War I on April 6, 1917. Patriotism ran high as local men joined the 72,000 men and 1,400 women from Arkansas who would serve in the war effort. An honor roll listed over 138 "brave and true boys" of Rogers in the 1919 town phone directory, and the majority of Benton County men served in the 142nd Field Artillery of the 39th Division of the National Guard.

But men were not the only citizens to serve in the war effort overseas. Vera Key grew up in Rogers where her father ran the War Eagle mill and later owned a store on the corner of First and Poplar Streets. After graduating from high school, Key attended the Centenary Hospital Training School for nurses in St. Louis. She worked as a nurse in Rogers, and then went to France in 1918 to assist in the military hospitals. Devoted to public service, Key, following her return to Rogers, organized the Garden Club of Rogers and helped establish the Benton County Historical Society and the Rogers Historical Museum.

On the homefront in Rogers, folks were also busy supporting the war effort. The federal government had established a National Council of Defense that applied social pressure to men who hung around pool halls or were considered "slackers" in order to encourage them to join the war effort. The like-minded Rogers City Council had earlier passed Ordinance No. 62, which prohibited "the keeping or running of pool, billiard and other gaming tables, shooting galleries or bowling alleys within the corporate limits." These laws also applied to young people, and Ordinance No. 64 specified it unlawful for "any person under the age of eighteen (18) years to loiter upon the public street, alleys or other public places . . . after the hours of 8 o'clock p.m. from the first day of September in any year to the 30th day of March succeeding, and after 9 o'clock pm, during the remainder of the year."

Troops leave their families behind as the Frisco takes them toward conflict during World War I. (Rogers Historical Museum.)

Around the country, there was a fear of the spread of Bolshevist doctrines, and the State of Arkansas responded to that real or perceived danger with Act 512, approved on March 28, 1919. The act declared it "unlawful for any person or persons, to write, dictate, speak, utter, publish or declare . . . or in any manner disseminate knowledge or propaganda which tends to destroy or overthrow the present form of government of either the State of Arkansas, or the United States of America." Ordinance No. 113, passed by the Rogers City Council on May 3, 1918, made an even stronger statement.

> If any person shall, at any time or place within this city during the time the United States of America is at war with any other nation, use any language within the presence or hearing of another person, or commit to writing or printing [anything that would defame the] United States of America, flag, standard, color or ensign . . . or the uniform of any officer of the army or navy . . . or use language disloyal or abusive in character and calculated to bring into disrepute the United States of America . . . .shall be deemed guilty of a misdemeanor.

The ordinance went on to say that "any person, who shall . . . publicly or privately, mutilate, deface, defile, defy, tramp upon, or cause contempt upon . . . any flag, standard or ensign of the United States . . . shall be deemed guilty of a misdemeanor." And, finally, no flag or symbol of any nation with which the United States was at war could be displayed.

In 1919, the war ended, and the men and women of Rogers who had served their country returned with a greater understanding of the world beyond their homes. The William Minter Batjer American Legion Post, organized in Rogers that same year, honored the first Rogers man to die in the war. The group's charter members included John J. Warren, Waddie L. Perry, Mace R. Phillips, McKinley Reddick, Will A. Blake, J.H. Creech, E.D. Cannon, LeRoy McGinnis, Walter Reddick, Clyde McNeil, Troley Spencer, John E. Applegate, T.P. Applegate, Harold Applegate, Howell Hodges, John Torbett, Troley Lynch, Mack Phillips, Harry Torbett, and Erwin Gilliard.

Although the war dominated much of American thought at the time, another major problem, one that was certainly closer to home, was the Spanish Flu epidemic that killed perhaps as many as 30 million people throughout the world in 1918 alone. The disease respected no one—as the saying went at the time, "The poor couldn't afford to run and the rich (who had the resources) never knew where to go to avoid it." In Rogers, schools, public places, libraries, and churches were closed. To avoid contact with the disease, masks were worn, phone booths were locked, and cashiers were provided with a finger bowl of disinfectant. The people of Rogers demonstrated true neighborliness and became unsung heroes in this deadly fight at home. Henry Matlock reminisced with the Rogers Historical

Vera Key was an active member of the Rogers community and served as a nurse in the military hospitals of France in 1918–1919. (Rogers Historical Museum.)

69

Museum staff about his mother, who helped in the soup kitchen of their church during that time. The women would make vegetable soup, take it to a quarantined house, knock on the door, and leave the food. Later, they would return to pick up the container that was washed and ready for the next delivery. Like many hometown heroes and heroines, Matlock's mother contracted the flu and died.

Rogers's water supply in the early years came mostly from cisterns prior to the construction of the first brick water tower in 1888. In 1900, a new steel water tower capable of holding 100,000 gallons was built; however, a water treatment plant was not installed until 1915, following the order of the Arkansas Department of Health. Impure water was thought to be a contributing culprit in the spread of contagious disease.

Health was important for the citizens of Rogers, and a number of ordinances addressed the issue of sewage, or waste management. Ordinance No. 61, which was passed in 1906, stated "that hereafter it shall be unlawful for any person, firm or corporation to connect, maintain, or keep connected any pipe sewer or other drain from any water closet, or toilet, or from any cesspool or septic tank, with any open sewer or other surface drainage on any street or alley within the corporate limits of the City of Rogers." Along that same line of thought, Ordinance No. 66 required "that all closets, backhouses or privys [sic] within the incorporate limits . . . shall be placed in a convenient place that same maybe [sic] in easy reach of the scavenger." The "scavenger" was hired to clean the privies for 35¢ each time.

The peddling of fresh fruits and vegetables, peanuts, soda pop, popcorn, notions, and trinkets on the streets or sidewalks of Rogers required the peddler to have a license. So too did those who sold fresh meat from wagons in quantities smaller than one-quarter of the animal. "Transcient" [sic] doctors who "peddled patent secret remedies or medicines, salves, or ointments" had to furnish a certificate from "some reputable medical college showing his degree of M.D." in addition to paying for a city license.

Predictably, other changes in Rogers's society reflected the times. On the national level, the Fifteenth Amendment to the U.S. Constitution, approved in 1870, gave all men the right to vote regardless of "race, color, or previous condition of servitude." The Arkansas Poll Tax, initiated in 1892 (and abolished in 1965), was the only registration process a man had to complete in order to vote, but its procedures, payment deadline, and cost effectively kept many African-American men in Arkansas from the voting booths. Almost 50 years later, Arkansas's women got the right to vote in the Democratic primaries of 1918. Women in 15 other states had already obtained the right to vote before the same right was granted to women in Arkansas, and full suffrage came with passage of the Nineteenth Amendment to the U.S. Constitution in 1919. This amendment forbade the denial or abridgment of any United States citizen's right to vote on the basis of gender. Prior to that time, each state had been allowed to decide whether to grant or withhold suffrage. Among the more interesting reasons cited for giving women the right to vote at the time were the following: "More girls than boys are being educated; Persons who train citizens should understand the

A poll tax was required in order to vote in Arkansas from 1892 to 1965. In 1881, Macy Sager was charged $3.70 in property tax, $1.70 in personal property tax, and a $1 poll tax. Sager was given separate receipts for the payments. (Tom Sager.)

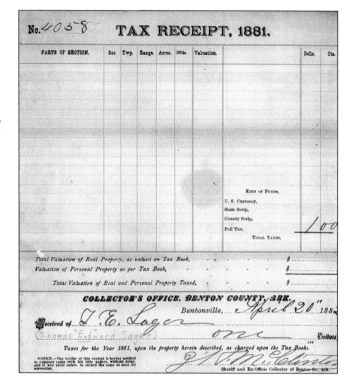

political duties of citizens, (most children are taught by women whether at home or in school) and; Both by nature and of necessity women have better moral habits than men."

Women in Rogers took an active role in many of the political issues of the day. Arkansas outlawed liquor in 1915, four years before the federal government legislated national prohibition. True to this conservative approach, Arkansas repealed prohibition in 1935, two years after the federal government abolished it. When Carrie Nation, a leading national abolitionist, came to town in 1906, her work had already been done. There were no open saloons to bust, so, according to a local story, Nation set an unsuspecting Frisco official straight when he dared address her with a cigar in his mouth and a hat on his head. In no uncertain terms, she divested him of both!

Arkansas became a better place to work for all as new laws were established to protect the rights of men, women, and children. In 1905, the hours of a worker in a sawmill were decreased to just 10 hours a day. In 1913, the Arkansas state legislature enacted a law that limited a woman to working 9-hour days, 6 days per week, for $1.25 per hour. A 1914 law protected children under the age of 14 from work except during their summer vacation and then only if they had four years of schooling. No child under 16 could perform dangerous work.

Children's welfare was viewed much differently at the turn of the twentieth century than it is today. The Children's Aid Society, along with other assistance

71

groups, operated a program from the late 1800s through the early 1900s that took indigent children from New York, bathed them, and provided them with Sunday clothes. The children were given a Bible and put on a train headed west in the hope of finding foster homes for them. Stopping in towns along the way, the children were lined up and presented to the local populace. Not all the children were actually chosen; some of the selected were lucky, others were not. Nearly 200 children were taken into homes in Arkansas, and at least 10 children were recorded as living with families in Rogers. It was the prevailing thought at the time that a child would adjust better to a new home if they had no vestiges of their past life with them, no tangible reminders of siblings, parents, or former homes. Thanks to the efforts of people such as Mary Ellen Johnson of Springdale and the Orphan Train Heritage Society, many of these orphans, now in their later years, have located a biological brother, sister, or other family member whom they might not have ever found otherwise.

Women continued to enthusiastically support education in Rogers. In 1902, the Mas Luz Club changed its name to the Women's Study Club, and in 1904 it created a library for the town from funds raised through various benefits. For a fee of $1.50 per year, a person could obtain checkout privileges for the library's 450 books. The library was housed over a period of time in several buildings, including private homes, the second floor of City Hall, and the Post Office building on Second and Poplar Streets. Much later, in 1933, the club would officially turn the library over to the "tender mercies" of the city with the

Leading citizens of Rogers met the Orphan Train in 1912 in front of the Hotel Main. The committee members include T.A. Winkleman, A.B. Stroud, Reverend O.R. O'Bryant, Henry Cowan, Mayor W.F. Rozelle, E.M. Funk, A.S. Teasdale, Dr. R.S. Rice, and S.S. Michael. (Jerry Hiett.)

The Mas Luz Reading Club, forerunner of the Women's Study Club, was instrumental in organizing Rogers's library. Pictured here are, from left to right, (front row) Julia Benedict, Mary Parks, Lulu Reardon, Mrs. A.M. Buckley, Mary Ellis, and Kate Ellis; (back row) Ora Lowry, Clara Latham, Sara —, Lizzie Shadel Haman, Mrs. "Doctor" Robinson, and Mrs. — Doescher. (Rogers Historical Museum.)

recommendation that a librarian be hired for $10 a month. Mary Parks was awarded this position and Julia Benedict served as the first assistant librarian. Mayor E.W. Vinson appointed Mrs. O.F. Mayfield, Mrs. E.W. Pate, Mrs. D.E. Merrill, Mrs. J.S. McLeod, Mrs. George M. Love, Mrs. E.C. Downer, and Mrs. Guy Russell to the first City Library Board.

The Minervian Club, organized in 1919, was the first Benton County Extension Homemakers Club. Members studied food, nutrition, health, gardening, poultry and dairy products, and any other subject that was related to the home or farm. This was a very active group that toured members' homes and pantries, noting the foods that had been canned. This stalwart group even built its own clubhouse in the 1930s. According to an interview with Zella Harris in the *Rogers Daily News*, the women, with the help of their husbands, gathered rocks for the building and bought lumber in Rogers that they paid for with the proceeds of various fundraisers. The Women's Progressive Club, organized in 1920, was another group that worked for the good of the community, developing fundraisers for various projects at the local schools. The club also worked hand in hand with the Rogers Rotary Club in providing holiday meals to families in need.

One Rogers woman in particular drew national attention. Much is written about Betty Blake, a Rogers native, and her romance and marriage to Will Rogers, the nationally known humorist, motion-picture cowboy, and political satirist. Betty was the daughter of Mr. and Mrs. J.W. Blake who lived at 307 East Walnut Street. J.W. ran a small sawmill, and his wife was a dressmaker. At the time of

Will Rogers and his wife, Betty (Blake), supported many worthy causes both on the national level and in Rogers. The couple shared a sense of humor for which Will was internationally famous. (Will Rogers Memorial Museums, Claremore, Oklahoma.)

Betty's marriage to Will Rogers in 1908, he was a vaudeville performer. His fame came later. Will Rogers did not actually spend much time in Rogers; however, when fortune came his way, he shared generously with many causes as well as with the town of Rogers. One-third of his donations to the Red Cross during World War I were given to the Rogers branch. He also donated money to help grade and put gravel on the downtown streets. Will Rogers is known for many famous quips such as "Every man has wanted to be a cowboy. Why play Wall Street and die young when you can play cowboy and never die?" and "I never met a man I didn't like." Rogers also said, "The day I roped Betty Blake was the best catch of my life." Famous though he was, Will Rogers was not the only humorist in the family. Betty Blake wrote the following tongue-in-cheek definition of an ideal husband in a special issue of the local weekly, which was purportedly written entirely for and by women:

> My Ideal Husband must be a man not too dark, or not too fair, not too fat, or not too slim, not too old or not too young, not too lazy or not too energetic to be out of place in Arkansas. I do not wish him so tall that he has to be folded up to insert him in the Opera House, nor so short that he hasn't the price of reasonable delicacies. He must be fond of onions and me to the extent of speaking kindly at least once every other Sunday

and must allow me the privilege of selecting my own hat. After long and painful waiting, I've come to the conclusion that the Ideal Man is the one who says, "let's marry." Then you can shake him or wed him as you may choose—or both I'm told.

Another national figure who, in this case, played an unusual role in national politics and in the town of Rogers was William Hope Harvey. Educated as a lawyer, Harvey spent most of his adult life promoting his belief in bimetallism, which advocated that gold and silver be used jointly as legal tender. His support of the silver standard and his book *Coin's Financial School,* written in 1894, won him the nickname "Coin." The name stuck. In 1896, Harvey supported William Jennings Bryan for president; when William McKinley won the election, "Coin" Harvey became disillusioned with the political system. He bought 320 acres of woodland in the Ozarks near Rogers on which he built a resort near Silver Springs. The resort was comprised of rustic hotels and a lagoon complete with a gondola and gondoliers. He named the resort Monte Ne, which he said was from the Spanish and Cherokee words for "mountain" and "water." The resort was marketed through the Monte Ne Investment Company, and building lots were sold to buyers all over the country, though most never used the lots they bought. In 1902, Harvey built a 5-mile railroad spur to Monte Ne from Lowell to encourage more travel to the resort. Since most roads were poor, Harvey also organized the Ozark Trail Association in 1913 for the purpose of improving roads in Arkansas and Missouri—though mostly for improving the roads to Monte Ne.

A man of great energy and vision, "Coin" Harvey was a lawyer, author, presidential candidate, bimetallist, and the creator of the resort at Monte Ne. (Rogers Historical Museum.)

Signs and obelisks with "OT" (Ozark Trail) marked these roads and some are still in existence today. Roy Webster, when speaking to the Rogers Museum staff in 1988, remembered that local folks would give directions to "South OT" rather than "South Highway 71."

With the advent of the automobile, families began to drive to vacation sites that were nearer to their homes and to stay for just short visits; the custom of taking a train to a resort for an extended vacation was no longer in vogue. At the same time that this change in tourism was occurring (which negatively affected Harvey's resort business), Harvey experienced other financial difficulties with union labor and the failure of both his newspaper and bank. Convinced that the fall of civilization was imminent, Harvey announced plans for the construction of a 130-foot-tall concrete obelisk, or "pyramid," that would contain a time capsule of twentieth-century culture and a message for future generations. He exhausted his remaining funds on the construction of an amphitheater and the obelisk was never built. The author of many books, a 1932 presidential candidate for the Liberty Party (created by Harvey and his supporters), and a political and economic activist, "Coin" Harvey died almost penniless.

Whatever the inspiration behind Harvey's dream, the "pyramid" (as the amphitheater is often referred to today) was an important part of the childhood of many who grew up in Rogers. Either while camping at nearby Camp Joyzelle or on a Sunday afternoon drive, kids enjoyed climbing on the pyramids and thinking

A favorite pastime for residents was to climb around the amphitheater's cement couches at Monte Ne. Local legend persists that cars, books, and other artifacts of twentieth-century culture are buried underneath. But historical evidence suggests that Harvey planned to put such items in the never-completed obelisk. (Shirley and Dean Park.)

Gold might only be found in small traces, but it can create big dreams. The Kruse Gold Mine in Rogers had the trappings of a big find but not the substance. (Rogers Historical Museum.)

about how future worlds would view us if Harvey had completed his pyramid and a time capsule had been buried. The amphitheater is now only seen in its watery grave beneath Beaver Lake on days when the lake reaches its lowest point. A visitor to Monte Ne can now only see Harvey's tomb, which was moved to high ground before Beaver Lake was filled, and the scattered cement remains of the old hotels.

Another early enterprise was based not so much on a dream as a vision. In the late 1800s, William Henry Kruse, the son of a local farmer, began having visions of a gold mine on Oak Street (near the later site of the Rogers High School and, perhaps prophetically, the Farmers and Merchants' drive-in bank). Kruse's visions were taken somewhat seriously as he had also had visions of the San Francisco earthquake in 1906 and the 1901 assassination of President William McKinley. He dreamed that there was gold at the base of an old apple tree on his father's farm, and after much searching, the tree was found. Kruse wanted to find the gold in order to distribute it and eliminate poverty. This was not a scam and local people were not asked to invest; however, images of *The Music Man* and its 110-cornet band come to mind when we picture the Rogers Cornet Band leading a group of townspeople, 30 workmen, and 7 two-horse scrapers to the mine to begin digging. The band played "Silver Threads Among the Gold" and "In the Shade of an Old Apple Tree." Nothing but gold traces was ever found, but with a mineshaft dug, smelters built, and a 100-foot tower hung with glowing lanterns erected in 1905, the enterprise had begun. According to company records, the mine kept eight or ten families in business until 1926, when the elderly Kruse died and the mine closed. Ironically, the hourly rate for the team of horses that worked the mine was higher than the hourly rate of the men. Kathleen Huber Garvin, the great-grandniece of William Kruse, still owns part of this land today.

Other gold excitement followed when a dig was undertaken to lengthen Walnut Street in the early 1920s. Former mayor Reverend J. Wade Sikes, sifting a handful of gravel used for the paving, declared, "Boys, there is gold in this stuff!" Assayers surmised that there were indeed traces of gold in the soil, but that this seems to be the case for most soil in the area. Scientific analysis aside, the streets of Rogers were pronounced to be "literally paved with gold!"

As the years went by, Rogers continued to witness a number of firsts. The first car ever seen in Rogers was brought in by Montgomery Ward on a Frisco freight car in 1897. In 1903, W.H. McMullin became the first person in Rogers to own an automobile, though it was destroyed in a fire less than a year later. Tom McNeil took advantage of the growing interest in cars and opened a Buick dealership in 1909 on Second and Poplar Streets, a site that is currently home to Las Palmas restaurant. The first Benton County Fair took place in Rogers in 1888, and a crowd of 10,000 people welcomed the Haggenback and Wallace circus to town in 1916. A contract for the first sewer system was let in 1909, and the first steel bridge was built over the White River in 1904.

Rogers telephone workers took all the calls in the late 1930s and early 1940s. They were a far cry from today's automated operators. (Sam Wood.)

Rogers was eager to be declared a "city of the second-class," and a special census in 1903 recorded 2,563 residents, more than was required for that designation. There was some confusion about the certification, however, and Rogers was certified a second time when Governor Jeff Davis signed the bill on April 17, 1903. The town was then divided into four wards along the lines made by Elm and Second Streets.

In time, the custom of moving the post office to fit the postmaster became unwieldy, and a permanent post office was built on the corner of Poplar and Second Streets in 1919. The first Rural Free Delivery (RFD) route began in 1904 with Jube Lee as the first mail carrier. The first city mail delivery started in 1911 with Algie Burns and C.T. Kirkwood as carriers.

The original Northwest Arkansas Telephone Company was sold to the Southern Telephone Company in 1910 and sold again in 1911 when that company purchased the Southwest Telegraph and Telephone Company. Shared party lines could sometimes lead to quarrels if users stayed on the line too long. Reception was not that good, and callers often needed to yell to be heard, especially if everyone on the line picked up during a call. Some early rules listed in the 1907 telephone book on the use of the telephone included the following:

> Always call by number.
> Do not use phones during storm.
> Vulgar or profane language over the lines not allowed.
> Don't hold the lines over five minutes.
> Don't talk to the operator!

The first city sidewalks in the business district were installed in 1903 and curbed with large limestone blocks quarried from the area where Lake Atalanta is today. Able-bodied men between the ages of 18 and 45 were required to help maintain the streets of Rogers or pay a fee of $1 a day in lieu of their labor—all had to register. Men who worked received $3 a day. This was not too much of a hardship, as no person was required to "labor on said streets, alleys, and public grounds more than six days in any one year." This 1917 ordinance also appropriated 25¢ an hour for the street commissioner to oversee the work.

The Interurban Trolley, which ran between Rogers and Bentonville from 1914 to 1916, was a handsome red coach trimmed in black and accented with gold lettering. The trolley ran ten times a day and could seat 130 passengers who paid 40¢ for a round-trip ticket.

When the Roger Public Schools System took over Rogers Academy in 1914, many townspeople became actively involved in the support of the schools. A.B. Stroud became a member of the school board in 1919 and promised to serve until replaced, which turned out to be 30 years later! The board's members maintained a watchful eye on all aspects of school operation, and for many years Dr. Guy Hodges looked after health matters; banker T.E. Harris advised on school

Large limestone blocks excavated from the Lake Atalanta site were used along sidewalks in downtown Rogers, as many a car bumper can testify today. (Ernestine Scott and Lorene Stephens.)

finances; J.O. Rand Sr., a wholesale grocer, checked on the food; and attorney C.W. Williams looked after legal matters.

Along with the rest of the country, Northwest Arkansas and Rogers suffered during the depression prior to World War I. At a time when banks were failing around the country, so too did the Bank of Rogers in 1914, and only a pardon from the governor kept the bank president out of jail. Local business failures and general hard times had left the Bank of Rogers holding bad loans. Due in large part to the failure of the Bank of Rogers, the Rogers school system struggled for solvency. The bank closed while holding $600 of the public school's money, and this loss, added to other financial mishaps, forced the school board in the fall of 1915 to charge $1 a month per child for the first two months of school. The remaining six months were free for all except high school students, who were required to pay $1 a month for each of the eight months. The community was encouraged to offer funds to help students who could not afford the tuition.

Churches also addressed the problem of personal poverty in 1901, and, as a result, the Rogers Relief Association was organized in 1916. The association later became defunct but was revived by local businessmen in 1931. G.P. Harbin was the group's first president; L.G. Sheddan was secretary; and Dr. P. Wakefield was in charge of relief work. A county Poor Farm made an effort to help the pauper inmates with 30¢ a day for all their needs including medicine. Administrators were given just so much money and took care of the people from those funds. The Poor Farm was later named the Benton County Home in 1907.

Businesses were active in Rogers even before the town was incorporated, but a formal structure to promote business was not in place until the organization of the

The charter members of the Rogers Rotary Club were Dr. Harry Peace, Tom McNeil, A.D. Callison, Dr. George Love, E.G. Sharp, and Erwin Funk. (Rogers Historical Museum.)

Board of Trade in 1903. J.W. Walker served as the board's first president; R.L. Nance as vice president; J.E. Felker as treasurer; and Dr. A.M. Buckley as secretary. Other members of this board were George D. Parks, T.B. Warren, and W.R. Cady. Walker was succeeded by J.E. Applegate a year later. The board initiated many downtown promotions but finally folded for lack of funds. Then in 1907, many of the members of the Board of Trade reorganized as the Rogers Commercial Club, with E.M. Funk as president, and took on the task of marketing Rogers's businesses. F.F. Freeman was the group's president in 1908; A.S. Teasdale in 1910; Frank Hardy in 1911; J.A. Dotson in 1912; Dr. George M. Love in 1914; and Perry Clark in 1915. There was very little activity on the part of the Rogers Commercial Club during the war years. In January 1917, the Rogers Rotary Club became the leading business organization with Perry Clark, Morgan McMichael, Erwin Funk, Dr. George Love, Ed Sharp, Clifford Fritz, and Ed Baker as its first board of directors. This club helped form the Rogers Community Club in 1921 with Vint Deason as its president. These groups were the forerunners to the Rogers Chamber of Commerce, which was organized in 1942.

A.O. Clarke is primarily responsible for the architectural ambiance of downtown Rogers. A self-made and self-taught architect with the firm of Matthew and Clarke of St. Louis, Clarke was brought to Rogers to work on "Coin" Harvey's Monte Ne resort buildings. Not all of his projects were completed at Monte Ne due to the downturn in the resort business; however, Clarke made Rogers his permanent home. Numerous outstanding commercial structures in Rogers, Bentonville, Eureka Springs, and Clarksville were designed by Clarke, and many of these buildings now appear on the National Register of

A.O. Clarke was the architect for many of the buildings in downtown Rogers. He also designed a number of the distinctive private homes in town. (Reagan family.)

Historic Places. Clarke's career also took him beyond the Ozarks and included work in places such as Cuba.

Both Clarke and his wife, Grace Emma Brownlee Clarke, were very community-minded citizens. Clarke was a member of the Rogers Rotary Club with an outstanding record of attendance, while Mrs. Clarke devoted much of her time to the beautification of Rogers with gardens, flowers, and other plantings. According to a report of the Woman's Progressive Club that refers to Mrs. Clarke's work, "She has made garden week popular; in every section of the city may be found shrubs and waste places planted to flowers where a few years ago only weeds and tin cans found a safe harbor."

Since downtown streets were still unpaved, one might have expected downtown buildings to be rudimentary in their architectural style. Rogers was most fortunate, however, as many of its early buildings were designed by Clarke and rivaled the architecture in much larger cities of the day such as St. Louis or Chicago. The most noticeable and consistent feature seen in buildings of the late 1800s is the quoin work above window arches and on the corners of structures. This use of solid, rusticated limestone block contrasts pleasantly with the surrounding brick construction. Dentil molding along the top facades is also evident on many downtown buildings. On sunny days cornice brick designs dramatize the play of shadow and light and add further dimensions to building facades. Various skilled brick masons worked with Clarke, including John, Zeke, and Frank Matthew; John Myler; and Myler's stepfather, C.R. Crowe, who would lay the brick streets of Rogers in 1924, almost 20 years later.

Among the more significant buildings Clarke designed in Rogers are the following structures: on the northwest corner of Second and Poplar, the Mutual Aid Building (built 1913), also known as the Progressive Life Building or Poplar Plaza and now occupied by Keith, Miller, Butler & Webb law firm; the Applegate Drug Store and First National Bank building (both built between 1905 and 1907), the current homes of Poor Richard's Gift and Confectionery and the Daisy Airgun Museum, respectively, at 116 and 114 First Street; on the northeast corner of Second and Cherry, First Baptist Church (1905), which later burned down (the new church is located at Eighth and Olive Streets); Central United Methodist Church (1908) at 307 West Elm Street and now named First United Methodist Church; Victory Theater (c. 1927) at 114–118 South Second Street; Rogers Wholesale Grocery (1907), now the Dollar Saver, at the northeast corner of Walnut and First Streets; Rogers High School (1911), currently the location of Regent's Bank, in the 500 block of West Walnut; the former Rogers City Hall (1929) at 212 West Elm; the Vandover Building (1909) at 119–121 West Walnut, now occupied by Benchmark Group and an earlier upstairs home to the Elks Lodge; and the Presbyterian Church (1915), of which Mr. and Mrs. Clarke were charter members, on Walnut and Fourth Streets (torn down in 1994).

Known by various names—Mutual Aid Building, Progressive Life Building, and the Poplar Plaza—this handsome structure is an A.O. Clarke design. (Marilyn Collins.)

Applegate's Drug Store, now Poor Richard's Gift and Confectionery, is one of the most richly appointed buildings in downtown Rogers. Mahogany counters and shelving gleam above marble-topped counters. Drawers still have their original ceramic knobs. Inlaid tile covers the floor, and the pressed tin ceiling is painted white and peach. Other Clarke-designed buildings of interest in the area include the Benton County Courthouse (built 1928) and Massey Hotel (1910) in Bentonville; and the Sunset Hotel (1929) in Bella Vista (burned down in 1999). Examples of private homes in Rogers designed by Clarke include the John E. Felker house (*c.* 1890), the C.W. Juhre house (*c.* 1910), the Walker-Duty house (*c.* 1920), and the H.L. Stroud house (*c.* 1910).

Many other residences of the late 1800s and early 1900s in Rogers have also managed to retain their architectural integrity. These include the Parks-Reagan house (*c.* 1898); the Hawkins house (1895), which is now part of the Rogers Historical Museum; the E.W. Vinson house (*c.* 1885); the Merrill house (*c.* 1895), the J.B. Myler house (*c.* 1885); the M.V. Deason house (*c.* 1890); the Ella Adams house (*c.* 1890); the J.A.C. Blackburn house (*c.* 1907); the E.J. Kruse house (*c.* 1910); and the A. Deason house (*c.* 1900).

An appreciation for the design and character of these early homes continues with their owners today, many of whom are restoring and renovating homes near the historic downtown area. A growing trend finds young professionals and retirees seeking out older homes and lofts above downtown stores to add a unique dimension to their lifestyle. Early storeowners often lived above their shop, but today's residents find the ambiance of the historic downtown living both relaxing and fun.

The John E. Felker house, built c. 1890 and located in downtown Rogers at Fifth and Cherry Streets, is one of many private residences that A.O. Clarke designed. (Marilyn Collins.)

Picking apples, then packing, processing, and shipping them, kept many local people in jobs during the late 1800s and early 1900s. (Rogers Historical Museum.)

Despite the retail growth in downtown Rogers during the late nineteenth and early twentieth centuries, the real action was taking place on the neighboring farms. Tobacco became a leading crop following the Civil War, and in 1887, 400,000 pounds of tobacco were grown in the county. Apple production, with its many related businesses, soon took the lead as the primary cash crop and was the main economic force during the early 1900s in Rogers and Northwest Arkansas. Benton and Washington Counties led the nation in the number of apple orchards, and Arkansas's winning apples gained national prominence at exhibitions in Boston, New Orleans, California, New York, and Chicago. Not surprisingly, Northwest Arkansas became known as the "Land of the Big Red Apple," and the apple blossom became the state flower in 1901. Strawberries, grapes, wild huckleberries, blackberries, cherries, peaches, and other fruits were also important but could not compare with the abundant apple crops. The apple appeared on the Rogers car tag until 1939 when the chicken replaced it on the tag and in the marketplace.

Some sources report that, prior to the Civil War, a wealthy Cherokee woman was responsible for the first apple orchards in Benton County and that she had slaves help tend her orchards. H.S. Mundell bought what was reported to be this woman's orchard and became the first large producer of apples in the county. The Arkansas Black was the most highly regarded variety of apple; it had dark red skin and yellow meat that had a "marvelous flavor," according to conversations between Roy Webster and the Rogers Museum staff. The apple matured late giving it a tough skin, which was good for cold storage over the winter months.

The industry grew in sales from $4,265 in 1880 to well over $1 million in 1918, and by 1901 Benton County was the leading apple-producing county in the nation. In the bumper crop year of 1919, 5 million bushels of apples in Benton County were sold at $1 a bushel. Local folks told of the long lines of wagons full of apples waiting at the Farmer's Union building to unload their bounties. Bentonville High School opened late that fall, as the students' help was needed in the orchards to handle the unusually large harvest.

Businesses handling apples and apple by-products flourished. Vinegar plants, dried-apple evaporators, canning factories, tree nurseries, makers of jams, jellies, and apple brandy, and cold storage companies were needed. The first brick evaporator was built in the late 1880s by R.L. Nance, who served in Rogers's city government, including five terms as mayor, as well as in the state house and senate. Local companies like the Teasdale Fruit and Nut Products, Hamilton Produce, Nelson and Rogers Canning Companies, Rogers Wholesale Grocery, Southern Fruit Products, David and Stephen Wing evaporator business, and the O.L. Gregory Vinegar Factory could individually handle from 800 to a 3,500 bushels of apples a day. The Gregory Vinegar Factory was the largest apple vinegar factory west of the Mississippi and was purchased in 1929 by Speas Manufacturing Company. Their payroll provided a stable income for local workers. Another early company was the Benton County Produce Company, founded by T.A. Winkleman in 1906. Winkleman was a successful entrepreneur who also helped local farmers find new markets for their "fancy white eggs," black walnuts, huckleberries, snap beans, cucumbers, and sweet potatoes. Other businesses necessary to the apple industry also thrived. Boxes and barrels were

O.L. Gregory Vinegar Company was the largest vinegar company west of the Mississippi. Here, barrels of vinegar await shipment on the Frisco railroad. (Rogers Historical Museum/Clarice Moore.)

Wing Brothers Evaporator kept busy drying apples and other fruit for shipment on the railroad. (Rogers Historical Museum.)

built, cold storage provided, and nursery stock cultivated. Growers, pickers, haulers, sprayers, and shippers were needed. The ice plant on Arkansas Street was a wonder to behold and was capable of producing 20 tons of ice a day to keep fruit cold during shipment.

Beyond the astonishing production figures was the sheer beauty created by these extensive apple orchards. Mrs. E.S. Warren of Rogers wrote the following description in a 1907 letter to a friend that was reported by Erwin Funk in the *Rogers Daily News*: "This country is nearly all orchard; a perfect forest of apple trees . . . [the trees are planted] in such long rows one cannot see the end of them; just long streaks of vivid red and green. And to think that all these apples have to be picked one by one! [The old saying] dollars don't grow on every bush [may not always be true—] but dollars do grow on every apple tree in this country."

With fruit such a valuable source of income in the area, it is easy to understand the reasoning behind City Ordinance No. 13, which was approved in 1891. The ordinance made it unlawful to "either willfully or maliciously cut, lop, girdle, or in any other manner injure any fruit, ornamental or shade tree, or knock down or injure any fruit, ornamental or shade tree; or knock down or carry away any fruit thereon."

Fruit was a featured item at the Benton County Fair, which was first held in Rogers in 1888. The event, however, suffered from a lack of sufficient funds and the fairgrounds were sold in 1908. Bentonville started a Fruit Fair in 1902 and soon became the sole sponsor of the county fair.

Diseases like San Jose Scale and Cedar Rust became problems for the apple crops, and cedar trees near orchards had to be cut down. Spraying was only partially effective, as the worms became immune to the insecticide over a period of time, and the process was very costly. Late frosts, heavy rains, and hot, dry summers were also the enemies of apple growers. Logan Leib, who was the first county agent and president of the Farmer's Union, often rode by buggy to visit farmers and help them with their farming problems. Leib recommended that farmers diversify their crops and income sources to safeguard against the failure of a single cash crop. Other agents soon followed and introduced cattle, hogs, and poultry as additional sources of income.

A poem sent to the Rogers Historical Museum by Ruth Sager Criswell sums up the plight of a "produce man." O.A.P. Oakley, a wholesale dealer of fruit, feed and produce in Rogers, wrote this tongue-in-cheek poem entitled "The Prayer of a Produce Man."

> Dear Lord,
> This is the end of a damn dull day,
> Tomorrow will go the same old way,
> Nothing to buy, nothing to sell,
> All the business is shot to hell.
> Nothing left but to pray for help,
> For money enough for wife and self.
> She wants a radio and a brand new car;
> Send something to sell and a market over par.
> Her idea of Heaven's a big buying spree;
> Please put a million apples on every apple tree.
> She wants seventeen dresses and a new fur coat;
> Just send the money, Lord, and I'll be the goat.
> She wants silk stockings to cover her legs;
> Please make hens that lay two daily eggs.
> She wants undies and overs, and a stunning new hat;
> Please make cows that give nothing but good butterfat.
> She wants what she wants, I'm calling for help,
> To corner the market and garner the pelf,
> And—
> I want a new tariff—I'm a good Democrat,
> But just do the rest Lord, and I'll not mention that.

Markets were quickly changing and in only 17 short years after the county's largest apple crop, dairy and poultry products became its new economic leaders. Carnation Milk had a factory in operation in Rogers by 1935, and the daughter of J.J. Glover in Cave Springs made money on her first flock of broilers in 1918. One could say that "the rest is history," but who could have known then of the powerful economic leaders in the years to come.

6. UPHEAVALS BETWEEN THE WARS

Many changes took place in Rogers in the era between the mid-1920s and the advent of World War II. While apples and their by-products were the area's chief economic force during the early 1900s, the poultry industry gradually shifted into this position. But prior to this change, the town and neighboring countryside began to celebrate the beautiful apple blossoms and the delectable fruit that brought riches to the area. Lovely girls dressed in gossamer and satin gowns rode in elaborate floats that were laden with crepe-paper apple blossoms, dipped in wax to preserve their fragile beauty. Towns, churches, civic organizations, and businesses in Rogers and beyond contributed to the festivities, and tens of thousands of people lined the streets for the annual Apple Blossom Festival parade. W.R. Cady, an orchard owner himself, introduced the idea of a festival in 1923 after being inspired by a peach blossom festival he had seen in Georgia. The festival started out as a hometown affair but quickly grew to encompass all of Northwest Arkansas. The Frisco railroad brought people from as far away as Joplin and Springfield, Missouri, and Fort Smith, Arkansas, clogging the streets with up to 35,000 people during the peak years before the festivals came to a close in 1927.

A festival court and queen, who was usually crowned by the governor of Arkansas, were selected, and a coronation ceremony kicked off the parade. Apple blossom fairies, "Sunshine Girls," and "Ozark Breezes" danced in costume as part of the program, while other costumed dancers, portraying trees and butterflies, represented nature. Tours of local apple orchards were arranged for visitors during the event and, coupled with the parade, drew a new tourist trade to Rogers. Margaret Smith Troutman, upon visiting the area in 1925, was invited to be a part of the "Radiant Red-Heads" and ride a float from Fayetteville. Her account in the *Benton County Pioneer* tells of her experience with nine other girls, all redheads, as they rode on the winning float pulled by six sorrel horses. (Many early floats were pulled by horses as car travel was not yet common.) The girls wore "brown sateen dresses" and held large bowls filled with apples that also spilled from a "gold" horn of plenty.

However, the worst fear of all outdoor event planners plagued the parade from the beginning. Rain, sometimes downpours, began to discourage parade planners and participants. Volunteers spent seemingly endless hours on the painstaking

Floats in the Apple Blossom Parade were elaborately decorated with crepe-paper blossoms. Girls carried bouquets of apple blossoms and wore flower-covered crowns. Thousands of spectators lined the streets to celebrate the number-one cash crop of the county at that time. (Rogers Historical Museum.)

process of making thousands of apple blossoms to decorate the floats only to see them wilt with the first few drops of rain. In addition, the apple industry was fast disappearing because of diseases and insects that grew to resist all attempts at eradication with spray.

With the increasing use of automobiles in the 1910s and 1920s, the need for paved streets became even more pressing. The four wheels of a car did not navigate the rutted dirt streets of Rogers as well as the four feet of a horse. An automobile ride could be quite rough before the streets were paved; horses, tied to hitching posts, would often paw the ground leaving the first "potholes" to lay in wait for an unsuspecting tire. John Myler, a brick mason who helped lay the brick streets in town, was already busy in Rogers working on downtown buildings as well as residences in the area. Impressed by Myler's work, architect A.O. Clarke hired him to build many of the buildings in Rogers that Clarke designed. Myler and Lee Adamson (Will Rogers's brother-in-law) also built the brick sewer plant west of in Rogers in 1916.

Bricks for the streets were brought in from Coffeyville, Kansas. The surface had to be prepared before they could be laid, so dirt was moved and leveled. The first streets to be paved were Walnut Street from First to Fourth Streets, Poplar Street from First to Second, and a block on First and Second Streets. Edith Erickson, in an interview with Casey Ward, recalls that there was a big celebration when the brick streets were completed in 1924. Faye Bottens Heins tells a story of how, upon seeing a few bricks left behind by the masons in the middle of the street in front of Callison's Funeral Home, her parents stopped to pick them up. The bricks were then heated on top of the family's stove, wrapped, and put at Faye's feet at night to keep them warm. The original bricks still surface many downtown streets.

City services continued to improve. The fire department—first organized in 1888 with volunteers, a hose cart, and some hundred feet of hose—moved into a new era when, in 1915, an American LaFrance fire engine was purchased. That engine was then replaced in 1919 with an even newer model affectionately named "Old Huldah." The department, known as the Rogers Hose Company No. 1, reorganized in 1922 and became the Rogers Fire Department. An invaluable collection of early firefighting equipment illustrating the department's history is housed in the fire station at 201 North First Street. Former fire chief Rick Williams collected most of the artifacts to preserve the department's history and to serve as an educational exhibit for schoolchildren and the public.

The police force in Rogers originated in 1881 with Marshal Robert Sikes as the city marshal; in 1906, Marshal J.L. Shinpaugh became the first officer to wear a uniform. The first request for a police car was vetoed by the city council in 1939.

First Street, looking North, Rogers, Ark.

In the early 1900s, the streets in downtown Rogers were still dirt covered, apparent in this view of First Street, looking north. (Opal Beck.)

However, a fully equipped police car was purchased for the department in 1946, and a second man was hired in 1947.

Water for individual homes was typically supplied by collecting rainwater in cisterns or by digging a private well on one's own property. In 1888, a group of town citizens led by J.A.C. Blackburn conceived a system to distribute water from an elevated brick tower through iron pipes from Diamond Springs to the town. The system was privately owned by various people, and it provided an inconsistent level of water that was often rusty. Purification, required by the state following the epidemic of 1915, brought more attention to the quality of this service. However, it was not until 1945 that the city took over the water system under the leadership of J.A. Ragsdale, Robert L. Vogt, and W.R. Vaughan, the members of the first water commission. Curt Vaughan was the first manager.

Other infrastructure improvements were also made in the Rogers area during this period. Arkansas Western Gas was granted the franchise in 1929 to furnish natural gas; the contract for Highway 71 between Rogers and Bentonville was let in 1929; and Carroll Electric became the first electric cooperative in the area in 1937.

By the 1920s, Rogers (Senior) High School was going strong with the junior high students meeting in the old Rogers Academy building. (The building was torn down in 1936 by Works Progress Administration workers to make room for Central Ward school.) Built in 1910, Sunnyside School served students living in the northeast part of town, and Maple Grove School was built on the old fairgrounds on South Arkansas Street in the 1910s. Money came from an unexpected source when, in 1923, the Ku Klux Klan contributed funds for a school playground and a park. Charles Baldwin was the superintendent of schools in 1922. Birch Kirksey served as the high school principal in 1924, and in 1932, he became the superintendent of schools. Florence Robinson was principal at the Academy building and later taught high school English.

In the 1920s the students of Rogers began an unusual springtime event as the town was sprucing up for the Apple Blossom Festival. Students dressed in rags—girls in bonnets and boys sporting mustaches—invaded the town as hobos and offered to do odd jobs from shining shoes to doing yard work. The money they raised went to support school activities and sporting events. In 1916, high school seniors built a section of the sidewalk in front of Rogers High School and inscribed their names on it for posterity. The students in that 1916 graduation class included the following: Joe Torbett, Clesson Cain, Bohart Cowan, Clice Daily, Robert Deason, Lee Shaddox, Harold Applegate, Mollyjo Williams, Josephine Howard, Ethal Deason, Nellie Steinbremner, Velma Collins, Maud Bowen, Alice Silvey, and Agnes Kokanour.

The consolidation of schools began in 1929 and continued into the 1940s. New Hope, Fairview, Hickory Creek, Lowell, Rocky Branch, Elm Springs, Oak Grove, War Eagle, Cottage Hill, Shady Grove, Pleasant Ridge, and Droke were just some of the one-, two-, and three-room schools scattered around the county at that time. These small, community schools were often the center of social activity for

Rogers High School was a handsome building where thousands of local young people studied, played, and made lifelong friends. The school system was blessed with a dedicated faculty that, even as late as the 1950s, worked the last two months of school for no salary. (Jerry Hiett.)

rural residents. Pie suppers, for example, were held at night to raise money for the schools. At these events, schoolgirls (or their mothers) would auction off homemade pies to the highest bidder. The lucky winner would not only get the pie but would get to share it with the young girl who baked it.

Named for the Droke family who settled in Benton County in 1856, the Droke school, located on Highway 71 between Rogers and Bentonville, was typical of these community schools. At Droke, the teacher would get to school early to stoke a potbellied stove so that the building was warm by the time the students arrived. The front entry hall served as a cloakroom for coats and jackets. The teacher's desk was on a platform that doubled as a stage in front of the classroom, and a side room off the stage was, in today's terminology, a multi-purpose room. In that room, the women of the community sometimes made soup for the children's lunch, costumes were changed for programs, and a nurse who came for regular visits used the room to check each child's head for lice or to give inoculations. Everyone hated the lice check since those children who were discovered to have lice were sent home feeling disgraced. Behind the school were two well-worn paths, one to the boys' outhouse and one to the girls', and a simple, child-propelled merry-go-round was the only playground equipment.

Christmas was a favorite time of year at the community school. Local men would cut and put up a huge tree reaching from the floor to the high ceiling, and

Excited children and townspeople lined the tracks when Santa Claus came riding into Rogers on the Frisco train in the late 1930s. (Sam Wood.)

students would create handmade decorations. Each child was presented with a bag filled with lots of hard ribbon-striped Christmas candy that usually stuck to the side of an orange that was also in the bag; sometimes there were chocolate candies with soft, white filling sharing the sack as well. The children sang Christmas carols and often put on a holiday play. Songs were sung at school throughout the year, and some favorites included "O My Darling Clementine," "My Old Kentucky Home," "Swing Low, Sweet Chariot," "Onward Christian Soldiers," "Where Have you Been, Billy Boy," "Bill Grogan's Goat," "K-K-K-Katy," and the songs of each branch of the armed forces.

Teachers were challenged by having to keep four levels of classes going at once. The older children helped the younger ones, and teachers often read stories aloud that kept everyone's attention. Elmer Russell, in an interview with the Rogers Museum staff, stated one major advantage to this system: "If you didn't get it the first time, you'd hear it again the next year." Teachers like Opal Beck, Bethel Hammontree, and Merle Haga were dedicated to their work. Though not all teachers in the system had earned a four-year college degree, they did provide a solid education to their pupils.

Limited playground equipment did not dampen the fun that could be had during recess. Kids played Red Rover, Crack the Whip, marbles, Tug of War, jacks, hopscotch, and jump rope, which was often accompanied by songs or chants. At home, children amused themselves with a variety of activities: hand-shadow action figures on the wall, croquet on the lawn, climbing trees, wading in the creeks, paper dolls, dominos, Chinese checkers, anagrams, and jigsaw puzzles. Radio programs in the late 1930s and 1940s such as *Just Plain Bill*, *Stella Dallas*, and *Lorenzo Jones* were daytime favorites, while shows such as *Only the Shadow Knows*,

Fibber McGee and Molly, Lum and Abner, Jack Armstrong, The All American Boy, and *Amos and Andy* were popular fare in the evenings.

The consolidation of country schools forever changed the nature of small, rural communities. People became more disconnected as the school bus carried the children and the focus away from the rural school to the larger, more modern schools in town. The rural school's role as a central community gathering place was soon replaced by the more structured PTA meeting that brought together parents and teachers who often lived outside the neighborhood. Faye Bottens Heins, a student at Droke, summed up this change in an interview with the Rogers Museum staff: "There is an old saying that if you take the school out of the community, you don't have a community. This certainly happened at Droke. Monthly parties soon ceased. The club dwindled and finally stopped altogether. There is no Droke community anymore and to most people, the name has no meaning." Students were also distressed. Barbara Harris Youree, another Droke student, recalls memorizing a poem at the time that began, "They talk of consolidation, of collecting the children in town." Although, in theory, better educational opportunities were offered through consolidation, a special part of Americana was lost forever.

Educators in the public schools made an indelible impression on their students and the broader community. One shining example of this is a story told by Arthur

Before consolidation, small rural schools were the focus of community life. (Opal Beck.)

Deason in 1987 to the Rogers Museum staff about superintendent Birch Kirksey, who ran a tight ship but was also interested in the well-being of each student. Kirksey was a strong advocate for the students who lived in the country, and he made sure that children were taken to daytime school events and that buses ran at night for evening programs. Arthur Deason described an incident that he remembered as a student when Kirksey assisted the basketball team when they were unable to get to their game in Springdale. "Mr. Kirksey said, 'I've got an old Studebaker sedan, a large one, and it will hold all nine of you players, if you want to go that way.' " Deason was asked to drive with caution because the car's brakes were not working just right. He was instructed to drive slowly and pull the emergency brake if he had to stop. The car was full of both girl and boy players. In trying to negotiate a sharp curve, Deason was unable to get to the emergency brake because girls, sitting two deep, were in the way. The car slid into the curb and hit a tree, shearing off the wooden spokes on the wheel. Kirksey was called, and he sent a taxi to pick up the kids and bring them home. Kirksey took the blame and had all the repairs made himself. To Deason's relief, he did not make the kids feel bad about the accident.

The downtown section of Rogers was growing as many businesses opened their doors in newly constructed buildings. The Rogers Wholesale Grocery Company offered a little bit of everything to its customers from Junge cakes, Crusader matches, Grandma's soaps, cereal, spices, and Fredrick Cigars. Z.L. Reagan was president; H.L. Stroud, vice-president; L.W. Searcy, secretary; C.A. Daniels, treasurer; and O.E. Gillum. The Rogers Creamery Building, owned by Harold Amos and situated on the corner of Elm and Arkansas, still displays ghost marks of the original sign on the side of the building. The Corner Landing Company Building, constructed in 1885 at 119 East Walnut Street, was later home to Watson's restaurant and now houses Vision Technology. The Cadman-Felker house at 624 West Walnut, now owned by the Cochran, Schneider & Croxton law firm, greets people as they enter the downtown historic district. The original structure was frame; brick was added later as well as porches on the east and west sides. Across from the old City Hall is the Model Laundry, which was established in 1928 and is still in business today. Another building familiar to townspeople was the home of the Harris Bakery Company, established in 1936 on 114 West Elm Street, where many folks remember buying HBC bread. Some faint lettering still remains on the building, but the company is now located at 2301 South First Street, where they provide bread to local markets under other labels.

One of the most well known of the downtown buildings is the Lane Hotel, which was constructed in 1928 for Gus Lane by G.F. Hentchell of Springfield, Missouri. Made of steel and concrete, the Lane Hotel was known as the first fireproof building in Arkansas. Architect John Parks Almand designed the building in Moorish and Spanish architectural styles, and a red-tiled, straight-barrel mission roof enhanced this 50,000-square-foot building. Mahogany carved beams in a floral style crisscrossed the lobby ceiling, and the fireplace, when lit, revealed a carved replica of St. George slaying a dragon. Many local residents

Two of the oldest signs in town are still quite clear on the Golden Rule and H.L. Stroud buildings on Walnut Street. (Marilyn Collins.)

fondly remember dining in the Orchard Room, which was added ten years after the original structure was built. In the early days, limousines would deliver passengers to the foot-wide steps leading to the broad terrace that was outlined with wrought-iron stanchions. Gala events took place in the ballroom, which was floored in Italian marble and boasted wrought-iron chandeliers overhead cleverly designed to also serve as fans. The hotel had many interesting and famous names sign its register, including Amelia Earhart, Jack Dempsey, and Will Rogers. Earl Harris of Harris Baking Company was the hotel's second owner, and in 1935 he changed its name to the Harris Hotel. In 1948, new owners renamed the building Hotel Arkansas. It closed in 1963 and reopened as the Defender's Townhouse in 1967 and served as a retirement home. Joe and Dera Keen purchased the property in 1977 and renamed the facility the Rogers Townhouse. Currently, the retirement home is known as Peachtree on the Lane, retaining the original owner's name as part of the signage.

Other buildings of note were constructed during the mid-1920s and early 1930s. The original Rogers City Hall, at Third and Elm Streets, was designed by A.O. Clarke and was dedicated in 1929. The Victory Theater on Second Street boasted red velvet curtains and an ornate chandelier in the lobby. Corinthian-style capitals were spaced along the theater walls. The theater presented *American Beauty* in 1927, and showed the first talking picture to the public in 1929. Prior to the film, an 11-member orchestra played, and there was great excitement as local patrons walked to the theater or arrived by car for this event.

Many Saturday afternoons were spent in the Victory Theater on Second Street. The Rogers Little Theater group has now restored this elegant building that was designed by A.O. Clarke. (John Mack.)

Continuing to chronicle the local news, the *Rogers Democrat* was purchased by the *Rogers Daily News*, owned by Erwin Funk, in 1929. Erwin Funk was an outspoken editor with a wonderful sense of humor and a very active observer of human motives. When asked by a young reporter, "Why do your readers love you and your paper?" Funk replied, "I am not interested in having my readers love me. All I ask is that they respect my opinions as honest, even if dead wrong—and pay cash in advance to get them."

As in earlier decades, however, the big story was taking place on the farms outside of the downtown area. In 1938, Benton County, which had led the country in apple production, became a national leader in broiler production. The poultry industry began on a rather small scale as farmers raised their own chickens, bought feed and supplies from different sources, and sold the chickens to any outlet they chose. In the Rogers area, a few early industry pioneers helped set the stage for future growth. O.A.P. Oakley's Rogers Egg and Poultry Company began shipping processed chickens by train as early as 1921, and the company was able to ship frozen chickens by 1925. Vick Will of Willhill Poultry Ranch near Rogers introduced the "Vantress Cross" chicken, which was bred in California, to

Northwest Arkansas in 1949, and "Arkansas White Rocks," as Arkansas broiler chickens were known, grew in national popularity.

Several changes beginning in the 1940s revolutionized this fledgling industry. Companies like Garrett, Tyson, Peterson, George, and Hudson Foods contracted with farmers and supplied them with baby chicks complete with inoculations, feed, and supplies as well as purchased the final product! Better strains of male breeders, mechanized feeding and watering operations, and shorter growing time all played a part in producing larger broilers. Automated lights produced four-hour "days" and "nights," which caused the chickens to start eating again each time the lights went on. Later, the introduction of the long brooder houses increased the volume of chickens grown. The practice of cleaning out the chicken houses after each flock was discarded in favor of cleaning out the houses only once every year or two, thereby saving both time and money. Heavier chickens were thereby grown faster, more economically, and more profitably.

The Rogers Municipal Airport soon provided the means to ship large numbers of eggs and chicks into Rogers and to ship the final processed poultry out to market. In 1921, Oakley Produce Company shipped 52 railroad cars of eggs and 52 cars of poultry from Rogers. In contrast, during the years of 1947 through 1951, 20 million baby chicks were flown into the Rogers airport along with eggs for hatching. The finished product was later flown to market.

Erwin Funk, longtime editor of the Rogers Democrat, *was an outspoken supporter of his community. This picture, taken in the 1910s, conveys his humor and enthusiasm. (Rogers Historical Museum.)*

Dr. William Jackson inspects some of the millions of baby chicks flown into the Rogers Airport for local farmers to raise, 1946. The finished products were then flown to market. (Rogers Historical Museum.)

Soon, larger brooder houses, like this one on the old Rife farm, helped turn raising chickens into an international business. (Rogers Historical Museum/Evelyn Rife and Sammie Evans.)

The milk and milk products industry followed somewhat the same pattern as the poultry industry. Local farmers produced milk mostly for their families and sold any surplus. The production of a gallon or two a day per cow was average, and the butterfat content was low. The cows were mostly "scrub" and not bred for high milk production. In 1935, Carnation and Pet Milk came into the county, and Kraft opened a cheese plant in Bentonville. Scrub cows were culled, and new breeds, feed, and management systems were introduced, increasing milk production from about 10,000 pounds per day to about 400,000 pounds a day. The Arkansas Poultry Federation, farmer's cooperatives, the Arkansas Farm Bureau, the Dairy Herd Improvement Association, and the Artificial Breeders Association, along with other local, state, and national organizations, contributed to these major industry improvements.

However, the economic growth of the early 1920s was disrupted and almost completely destroyed by natural disasters, government mismanagement, and the bank failures that led to the Great Depression. Although the Depression affected the entire country and much of the world, Arkansas had its own special problems and concerns that compounded the matter.

First came the Great Flood of 1927 that sent the Mississippi, Arkansas, and White Rivers roaring from their banks, destroying crops, property, livestock, and homes along the way. The unfortunate timing of this spring flood made planting nearly impossible that year, and counties that depended on a single cash crop for the majority of their income were hurt the most. The rivers remained at flood stage from late April into May. Not only was personal property severely damaged,

The milk industry grew alongside the emerging poultry business. Lewis Brewer is in the lead of this convoy of Carnation trucks. (Rogers Historical Museum/Paula Smith.)

but so was the state's infrastructure of bridges, levees, roads, highways, and railroad beds in the affected areas.

The stock market crash of 1929 caused bank closings and the loss of savings for businesses and individuals alike. Elmer Russell related a story that played out similarly in many families. "My father and mother had some money in the Bank of Rogers. When it went broke, I think my father was left with 17 cents in his pocket. But he was a very energetic man. He knew how to farm and knew how to buy cattle, trade horses, butcher beef and sell it . . . . We always ate real good but didn't have a lot of money. There were many people that went to work for the WPA. There just weren't any jobs for them, but my father managed to make it." Another story told of a man who was out duck hunting with $14 in his pocket. By the time he arrived home, his life savings, held in the bank, were gone and all he had left was what was in his pocket. Such an unexpected jolt to a person's life and means of support was devastating to many. In just a day, the world was turned upside down.

Locally, people made do in ways that are unheard of today. Ernestine Scott and her sister Lorene Stevens told how thread was unraveled from rags to mend usable clothes and to sew on buttons. Home Demonstration Clubs helped women come together to can vegetables and meat when available. Farmers cut wood from their land and sold it, and broken items were mended and used again. If sheets wore out in the middle, the two sides were sewed together; when a collar frayed, the collar was turned over and the other side used. All in all, people made do as best they could.

Compounding these problems, another natural force struck the land. A severe drought in 1930 burned crops, leaving very little food for people or their livestock. Great clouds of dust from drought-stricken prairie lands to the west blew across Arkansas, drying and covering everything in their path. One stretch of 100 days saw no rain in the state. During this time, many people headed to California, which was, in their minds, a mecca of green farmlands and plenty for everyone. John Steinbeck's *The Grapes of Wrath*, written in 1939, graphically depicts the plight of families facing the sometimes 110-degree temperature of the desert and the poorly developed roads over the mountains on this treacherous journey. A hostile welcome often greeted many of these pilgrims. Californians did not want an influx of people to take their jobs or add to their own economic burdens. As time went by, more and more families who endured the enormous hardship of getting to California were turned away at the border.

Rogers shared in the nation's misery. The loss of family land, often passed down through many generations, was probably most heartbreaking of all. Landholders, unable to pay their taxes or meet mortgage payments, lost their homes to a bank's foreclosure. Schools were hard hit since their money had also been kept in the banks, and the long tradition of local school control had to be given over to the federal government. With a debt of $32 million by 1932, education in Arkansas came to an almost complete stop. Teachers were put on the relief roles through the Federal Emergency Relief Fund (FERF), which later

Lake Atalanta was constructed in the mid-1930s as part of a WPA project in Rogers. The dam is under construction in this photograph. (Sam Wood.)

became the Works Progress Administration (WPA). Programs quickly labeled with accompanying acronyms flowed from the federal government to help relieve the widespread economic and unemployment problems in the state and across the country. The Public Works Administration (PWA) put skilled laborers to work building post offices, streets, and other construction projects; the Civilian Conservation Corps (CCC) hired young people for forestry work; and the Civil Works Administration (CWA) came up with "make work" jobs for people to do. Bureaucracy of this size was by nature inefficient and often held to high ridicule by those it was intended to help.

The state also endeavored to increase funds by legalizing and taxing hard liquor; dog races became legal in West Memphis; and Hot Springs again held horse races. Each of these activities provided a means of additional tax dollars.

Locally, the Rogers Relief Association (RRA), first organized in 1909, was revived in 1931 and became instrumental in accessing some of the Red Cross funds from World War I deposits that were being held by defunct banks.

One WPA project that took up a considerable amount of meeting time for the mayor and city council members during the 1930s was the construction and damming of Lake Atalanta (pronounced by local folks as "Atlanta"). The 100-acre site selected for the lake was owned by O.L. Gregory and named for his wife, Atalanta. The city entered into a contract with Gregory on August 18, 1936, to purchase the land. Mayor E.W. Vinson appointed Earl Harris, J.O. Rand, Harry B. Watson, and Jeff Duty to investigate the purchase of any additional land needed for the project, and D.W. Ogden was appointed to oversee the work for $2.50 per day. Earl Harris was later appointed as contract agent for the project and reported to the city council on all monies spent and current progress on the dam. Four thousand dollars needed to be raised beyond what the Lake Fund could cover. The city presented a deed of trust with the lake property as collateral to Wayne Stone, A.D. Callison, and Earl Harris. Following the payment of the debt, the trustees would then re-convey the lake property back to the city of Rogers.

Various other means were used to raise money. Tickets at $1 each, entitled "the holder to a free ride on the lake; also a chance to guess the exact time the water would flow over the spillway. The correct guess entitled the holder to the title of 'Commodore' of the Lake Yacht Club." There was also a charge of "50 cents per day for fishing; $5.00 per year for motorboat, or $1.00 per day; rowboat $2.50 per year or 25 cents per day" and a "limit of 10 legal [fish] of which not more than 5 bass (while in season) may be caught; not to use more (than) 2 rods or poles." A "charge of 10% be made in addition to the regular boat fee to all persons carring [sic] passengers for hire and that they shall have a life perserver [sic] for each passinger [sic]."

Other matters before the city council during this time were petitions from residents requesting "relief from dust" by oiling the streets. The council was amenable to this, as property owners had to pay the invoice price for the oil. Concern for safety at the corner of Eighth and Walnut Streets was relieved by the placement of one reflector sign reading "stop" and another reading "danger" to prevent crashes at this intersection. The Second and Walnut Street intersection was handled with a "stop and go" signal, and U-turns at First and Walnut and at Third and Walnut were prohibited.

In 1935, Mrs. O.F. Mayfield, the chairman of the City Library Board, requested that the salary for the city librarian be raised from $10 a month to $15. The library was also granted permission to stay open on Thursday evenings from 7 p.m. to 9 p.m.

In May 1940, the clerk read an ordinance to prohibit the sale of beer and wines on Sundays. One of the councilmen, who was against the passage of this ordinance, said, "There is a couple of places in town that need to be closed but if a place is good enough to sell beer on Mondays it is good enough to sell beer on Sundays." He made a motion that this ordinance be tabled. The motion received a second and was tabled by the council.

As this era in the history of Rogers came to a close, the hardships experienced by both residents and their land still lingered and would come to have a lasting effect. Wars, both home and abroad, which had been a dominant force in decades past, faded in comparison to the personal memories of both the good and bad times that were had in the 1920s and 1930s. However, modernization was waiting in the wings until the rumblings of another world war brought it to center stage in Arkansas.

7. A New World View

Reeling from the effects of the Great Depression, Benton Countians began to rebuild their economy and get on with their lives. Although Northwest Arkansas was not as hard hit as areas that were dependent on a single-product economy or the parts of the nation that were more directly affected by the stock market crash, tough times had intensified for local farmers and there were fewer non-farm job opportunities.

The seeds of war, planted at the conclusion of World War I, grew in the mid-1930s as Italy, Germany, and Japan looked beyond their borders to neighboring countries for expansion. By 1937, these nations formed a coalition called the Axis Powers. That same year in Rogers, J. Wesley Sampier helped to organize Battery F, 142nd Field Artillery unit. The draft followed with the first registration on October 16, 1940. Many not already serving in the National Guard unit joined the different branches of service as individuals.

The early dew had not yet dried on the morning of January 16, 1941, when the Rogers unit moved out for Fort Sill, Oklahoma. Joining up with the Fayetteville batteries, they became part of the 18th Field Artillery Brigade. Special Frisco cars sat on the tracks that night waiting to take the men, not traveling in the convoy, to Oklahoma. An empty feeling fell over the town as the men pulled out. The unit was allowed to return to Rogers in November 1941 for the dedication of the National Guard Armory on South Eighth Street. A month later, on December 7, 1941, Japan bombed Pearl Harbor, thrusting the United States into World War II.

Soldiers from Benton County were placed with various units around the world, holding assignments that included North Africa, Italy, Sicily, France, Austria, Czechoslovakia, Germany, Belgium, and Alaska. Over 1,800 men and women from Benton County served as part of the nearly 200,000 troops supplied from the state of Arkansas. Whether wading ashore on the bloody beaches of Normandy or serving in other conflicts—on the front lines or in the rear echelons—the men fought bravely; some received decorations for their valor. Benton County grieved the loss of 120 men killed in the line of duty. Blue stars adorned the windows of homes where a family member was serving in the war, and gold stars indicated where one had paid with his life. The town also erected a tribute in Frisco Park honoring the servicemen and women of World War II.

Eager recruits enlist for World War II in front of the Victory Theater on Second Street. Soldiers stand at attention near the patriotic posters that read "Buy a Share in America" and "For Freedom's Sake, Buy War Bonds." (Rogers Historical Museum.)

Folks at home also made sacrifices. Volunteers served as air raid wardens, aircraft spotters, and performed other duties for the Civil Defense Administration. Mayor R.L. Vogt served as a captain of the Rogers Home Guard. Women worked with the Red Cross making surgical bandages or knitting sweaters, gloves, and helmet liners. Both adults and schoolchildren collected scrap metal. In 1942, Birch Kirksey, the superintendent of schools in Rogers at the time, let school out early so the children could participate in a special promotion conducted by the Rogers Theater, in which 5 pounds of scrap metal were accepted for the price of a movie ticket. Families planted and carefully tended Victory Gardens. Food grown in these gardens had to be preserved, and so canning kitchens were set up with home economics teachers giving tips on the proper use of pressure cookers.

Food, sugar, fuels, and shoes were on the list of rationed items during the war. Each person was allowed only one pair of shoes a year, and even Christmas lights were kept to a minimum to conserve energy. These were accepted sacrifices of the day—anything to help the war effort. Illegal money was made by some on the black market by supplying hard-to-get items. In an interview with the *Northwest Arkansas Morning News*, Opal Beck told of a swindler who sold white sand from New Mexico as sugar on the black market. But he was "long gone" before his deception was discovered.

The Minervian Club, one of the Benton County Home Demonstration Clubs, took on various projects to aid the war effort, including making hundreds of

People at home did their part to support the war effort, as well. For example, the Minervian Club, depicted in this 1930s photo, used pressure cookers to can vegetables grown in Victory Gardens. (Rogers Historical Museum.)

cookies to send to Battery F. The club and many other groups throughout Benton County also took on a very unusual project. Surplus cotton, unable to reach overseas markets during the war, was sent to 17 Southern states to be made into mattresses for people with insufficient income to purchase their own. With an incredible effort 2,000 mattresses were produced in the county, and both men and women got into the action as a 50-pound pile of cotton and 10 yards of ticking were converted into mattresses—one after another. Lila B. Dickerson, a home demonstration agent, led the process. The women made the ticking, and the men beat lumps out of the cotton for a smooth mattress. The finished product was said to compare quite favorably with store-bought ones.

Workers were needed in abundance for the war effort. Women joined the workforce outside the home, many for the first time. Arkansas received only 1.16 percent of defense spending, which resulted in many people leaving the state to find defense jobs elsewhere. Arkansas towns that were granted contracts were often ill prepared to handle the surplus population and the needs of the new workers. Some local workers, recruited to help in the war effort in other states, returned after the war, but many stayed in their newly found homes.

Two relocation camps were established in the state of Arkansas. Sentiments ran high against foreigners, especially those of German and Japanese descent, though German detainees were typically more welcome by local people, many of whom were of German descent, than were the Japanese. Additionally, the bombing of Pearl Harbor provoked strong feeling against the Japanese. Laws enacted in

Arkansas forbade Japanese from owning land in the state. Their children were unwelcome in the schools, and birth certificates were not issued for children born in the camps. Many of these laws were later declared unconstitutional.

The war ended in Europe on May 7, 1945, with the surrender of Germany. Following the atomic bomb strikes on Japan in early August, Japan surrendered on August 14, 1945. Church bells rang, horns blew, and fire sirens rent the air declaring that the war was over. People took to the streets to celebrate, churches held special services, and shops closed in honor of the victories in both Europe and Japan. Opal Beck provided an apt description of life after the war in the *Northwest Arkansas Morning News*:

> All these events were bringing us into the 50s, which really marked the beginning of the phenomenal growth of our town. People were more mobile, highways were being built, and air travel was becoming very common. All these things were an outgrowth of the war experiences. So even though the 40s were sad in so many ways, the technology learned in the war years brought about improvements and growth in the industrial field, medical world, and agriculture. Many of our young men and women who had never traveled beyond Benton County and our State were exposed to cultures and customs from . . . all over the world.

Some returned to the family farms, many of which were undergoing dramatic changes. The mechanization of farm equipment decreased the need for the number of workers necessary prior to the war, and many veterans, after seeing the world and gaining new skills, soon sought other means of employment.

A happy event brought the 1940s to a conclusion in Rogers as 78 couples reaffirmed the wedding vows they had taken 50 years earlier. In front of the Harris Hotel, these couples celebrated their golden wedding anniversaries in a special service conducted by Reverend J.H. Martin, a former pastor of the Rogers Church of Christ. A parade including vintage automobiles followed the ceremony, as did a reception boasting a wedding cake presented by Roy Webster of the House of Webster in Rogers.

As life in Rogers began to settle down in the post-war era, the poultry industry remained strong. Tyson Foods had purchased its first farm in the area in 1942, and the Rogers Airport played a significant role in the industry's success in all of Northwest Arkansas. The first "Operation Chicken Haul" arrived at Rogers Airport in 1947, delivering 40,000 baby chickens that were loaded on trucks and deposited at brooder houses throughout Northwest Arkansas. The chicks had to be unloaded quickly as air ventilation ceased when the plane landed. Some 20 million chicks were flown in between 1947 and 1951. Hastings Hatchery, the largest hatchery in the world, opened in Rogers in 1948 with a capacity to hatch 3 million chicks annually.

The Airport Association, formed in 1945, helped spark local interest in aviation and the airport, and even women and children became involved. The Rogers Women's National Aeronautical Association was organized in 1947. That same

Couples celebrated their golden wedding anniversaries in a special ceremony held on the steps of the Harris Hotel. (Rogers Historical Museum.)

year, the first Wing Scout Troop in Arkansas formed in Rogers under the leadership of Doris Larimore and Louise Jefferson.

"Fly-In Day," which began in 1948, became a very popular event at the airport with as many as 50,000 people in attendance during its peak in the 1950s. C. Jimmie Carter was then president of the Rogers Airport and the event's chairman after having succeeded Earl A. Harris, the corporation's first president. Carter's board included Ralph McGregor, vice president; Frank Van Meter, secretary/treasurer; and members W.C. Putman and Earl A. Harris. Carter became so identified with the Rogers Airport that he was honored by the city council of Rogers. On April 15, 1975, "Councilwoman [Opal] Beck introduced Resolution No. 301, which was made to honor C. Jimmie Carter and . . . change the name of Rogers Municipal Airport to Rogers Municipal Airport/Carter Field. . . . Motion was made by [J. Wesley] Sampier and seconded by [John R. "Skip"] Gregory that this Resolution be adopted. All members voted aye." In accepting the honor on May 22, 1975, Carter made the following remarks:

> I consider this a great honor to have bestowed on me by the people with whom I have lived and worked for over forty years. "But no man walks alone." I accept this honor with sincere humility, but "I did not walk alone." No one could ever hope to have more cooperation than I had in whatever I may have accomplished in the development of the Rogers Airport to where it is today.

C. Jimmie Carter (left) looks over the runway expansion plans for the airport with contractors. Carter was very active in the growth of the airport. The field was renamed in his honor—Rogers Municipal Airport/Carter Field. (Maurice Kolman/City of Rogers.)

New non-agricultural industries began to move into Rogers and the surrounding area in the late 1940s and early 1950s. Among those companies was Munsingwear, which had its home offices in Minneapolis, Minnesota, and opened a plant in Rogers in 1947. The company produces hosiery and underwear items. Local people were trained for this new employment opportunity while the plant was under construction. All the nylon hosiery under the Munsingwear label was made in Rogers and Bentonville at that time.

In 1951, H.F. Pelphrey and Son Company, a California plant for processing rabbits, took over the Rogers Can building on Arkansas Street. The company consisted of three divisions: Pel-Freez Rabbit Meat, Pel-Freez Biologicals, Inc., and Pel-Freez Fur.

Wendt-Sonis Company began planning for a branch on North Thirteenth Street in Rogers in 1953, and the production of solid carbide or carbide-tipped tools began in February 1954. Local workers were hired and trained to produce tools for automotive plants and aircraft plants—any plant that machined metal, plastic, paper, or wood was a potential customer.

The move of 100 families from Plymouth, Michigan, to Rogers by Daisy Manufacturing Company probably had the most far-reaching socio-economic effect on the community of any of the new companies. In the late 1800s, the Plymouth Iron Windmill Company in Plymouth had produced windmills for farmers, but with the advent of more readily available electrical service, windmills declined in sales. The company's focus radically changed when, in 1888, Clarence Hamilton showed Lewis Cass Hough, the company's treasurer and manager at that time, a gun-like invention that shot round, lead ball–sized BBs, and after a few test shots, Hough declared the invention a real "daisy"—a name that stuck with the airgun through the years. After much discussion, the company's board agreed to produce a metal version of the gun to give to farmers as a gift when they purchased a windmill. Charley Bennett was hired as a salesperson, and on his first sales trip to Chicago, the hardware giant Hubbard, Spencer, Barlett and Company ordered 10,000 airguns! It took six months to fill the order. Plymouth Iron Windmill Company had discovered a new market that better fit the times and, in 1895, renamed the company the Daisy Manufacturing Company.

In 1957, Daisy purchased property in Rogers that was held by the Benton County Nursery on Highway 71. Garner-Larimore Construction Corporation, owned by Darrell Garner and F.G. "Larry" Larimore, were awarded the contract for constructing the building. They cleared the site, and nine months later, in July 1958, the plant opened. Daisy hired over 400 local people to work in their plant making airguns, and the impact of a $2.5-million payroll helped to trigger growth in Rogers. Highway 71 was just a two-lane highway and the paving on Dixieland Road went only as far as Cypress Street when Daisy came to town.

Daisy employees from Michigan were, for the most part, Republican and many were Catholic—not the norm for Northwest Arkansas. However, these new

Daisy's first advertising poster, printed in 1895, exhausted the company's advertising budget for that year. This is one of two numbered, collectible posters released by the new Daisy Airgun Museum on First Street in Rogers. (Daisy Airgun Museum.)

111

arrivals made a concerted effort to blend in and become a part of the community. They strongly supported the Rogers Chamber of Commerce with their memberships, joined civic organizations, and became a part of local churches. Daisy's policy, when possible, called for purchasing supplies from local companies, such as office supplies from Shofner's, clothing from Stroud's, office furniture from Moser's, and so forth. The Rogers Post Office, perhaps, felt the greatest impact from Daisy's arrival in town. There was no United Parcel Service at that time so all Daisy products were shipped through the Rogers Post Office on Poplar Street, increasing their volume significantly. When the Rogers Post Office was later moved to Walnut Street in 1961, a $100,000 donation by the Hough-Kimble Foundation, which was chaired by Cass Hough of Daisy, provided much of the necessary renovation funds for a new home for the city library. The library moved from the City Hall building to the post office's former Poplar Street location in 1964.

Cass Hough was executive vice president of the company when Daisy came to Rogers, a position he held until 1986, Daisy's centennial year. (Daisy counted its anniversary from the 1886 date when Markham Air Rifle Company first made a wooden air rifle. Daisy later purchased Markham.) Several leaders followed Hough, each instituting their own management styles. Eventually, the company began to outsource parts and moved their assembly work to Neosho, Missouri. Daisy now maintains only its corporate offices on Second Street in Rogers. The only current operation at the plant is the production of BBs.

The Daisy Airgun Museum, housed in the old First National Bank building on First Street, is located adjacent to Poor Richard's Gift and Confectionery in the restored Applegate Drug Store building (on the left). (Marilyn Collins.)

Nostalgia for Daisy products still has a strong place in the hearts of the people of Rogers as evidenced by the permanent collection of Daisy airguns and memorabilia on display at the Daisy Airgun Museum, which opened in 2000 in historic downtown Rogers. The museum offers a complete line of Daisy products for purchase as well as historic posters and several commemorative and collectible airguns.

International events at the time evoked responses—sometimes emotional—close to home. As before, the seeds of one war spawned the birth of the next, and Rogers citizens were brought into the fray once again when the People's Republic of Korea (North Korea) invaded the Republic of Korea (South Korea) on June 25, 1950. In Rogers, Battery F of the 142nd Field Artillery reorganized into Battery C, 936th Field Artillery Battalion, which then became a part of the U.S. Army headed for Korea. Once again a troop train left Rogers carrying our young men toward battle, and many of the troops from Rogers went on to serve on the front lines in Korea. Captain Douglas E. Morrow from Rogers was one of two men killed from Benton County. In January 1952, the first group of National Guardsmen returned home, though the agreement signed on July 27, 1953 to end the conflict left a still-divided Korea.

Only a year later, the aftermath of World War II developed into another combat situation, this time in Vietnam. In 1954, President Dwight D. Eisenhower pledged American support to South Vietnam. The ensuing war was an unpopular one that was fought around conference tables in Washington, D.C. and on the

Soldiers of the Rogers C Battery, 936th Field Artillery Battalion, take a moment to relax at Camp Carson, Colorado, before being shipped off to fight in Korea. (Rogers Historical Museum/JoAnna Richards.)

This memorial plaque honoring veterans of the war in Vietnam is located at the Rogers airport. Its inscription is printed below.

streets of the United States, as well as in the rice paddies and jungles of Vietnam. The National Guard unit in Rogers was not activated for Vietnam, but individuals from Benton County did serve. The conflict ended with the signing of the Treaty of Paris in 1973. Over 50 individuals, corporations, and organizations provided a memorial at the Rogers airport in tribute to those who served in Vietnam. Its inscription reads as follows:

> This memorial was erected in memory of the young individuals who went to war as kids and lost their youthful dreams, and some their lives, for a cause—freedom and honor—and came back as men with the horrors of war instilled in every fiber of their being and were never given the respect and honor they so dearly deserved from the public or the United States government. God will one day judge our actions. Until then, He will shine on the lives of each veteran now and forever more because He was with each of them in Vietnam. He is the only One that truly knows what they went through and are living with each day.

Racial unrest added to the turmoil that swirled through much of Arkansas and the country during the 1950s and 1960s. This unrest had less of a direct impact on Rogers and Northwest Arkansas than on other areas of the state in which the African-American population was greater. The riots that occurred in Little Rock over the integration of schools was not repeated in Rogers, as there were no minority students living in town. However, following the Supreme Court ruling in May 1954 that segregation was unconstitutional, nearby Fayetteville became the first school system in the state to integrate. Prior to that time, minority students had been bused from that city to Fort Smith to attend school.

Governor Orval E. Faubus, a six-term governor who served from 1955 to 1967, presided over the era of desegregation in Arkansas. It was his defiance of a federal desegregation order in 1957 that led to the well-known school crisis in Little Rock and set the tone for the South's white resistance to integration. Public opinion polls in the state indicated that a majority of white Arkansans were in favor of segregation. In predominately white areas, where there was little or no social interaction between races, prejudice arose mainly out of habit rather than from negative personal contact with members of the minority. However, with the broad national media coverage, the integration of Central High School in Little Rock became indelibly stamped on the minds of Arkansans and Americans alike.

The Civil Rights Act of 1964 ended segregation in public places, including bus stations, water fountains, and restrooms. "Whites only" and "Colored only" signs were removed. The lunch counters of Greenville, North Carolina, and the buses of Montgomery, Alabama, as well as confrontations in other states, however, kept most of the struggle for integration elsewhere. Ratified in 1964, the Twenty-fourth Amendment banned the poll tax, long a deterrent to minority voting in federal elections, and the Supreme Court banned it on the state level in 1966. The reaction of Arkansas voters to this political turmoil was in part responsible for the election of Winthrop Rockefeller in 1966 as the first Republican governor in Arkansas since 1874. Rockefeller realized the importance of seeking black votes, which helped give him a victory of 50,000 votes over his opponent James Johnson, who ran on a racist platform.

At home, civic-minded residents began making plans for a hospital in Rogers. Roy Vaughan, the president of the chamber of commerce, led the early planning stages in 1947. The project received an important boost with the donation of funds by the Rice family in 1948 to purchase 16 acres of land on which Rogers Memorial Hospital was built. Although great support was given to fulfilling the dream for a local hospital, it became evident in just a few months that help was going to be needed to operate a profitable facility.

In January 1951, the hospital came under the direction of the Sisters of Saint Dominic whose motherhouse was located in Springfield, Illinois. Sisters Rita Rose, Mary Robert, Mary Rupert, Marie Celine, and Mary Amata were the first leaders of the management team. The first administrator was Letta E. Bracken, RN; the first chief of staff was Dr. Hollis H. Buckelew; and the original board members of the Rogers Memorial Hospital Association were Kale M. Fones Jr., president; Newt L. Hailey, vice-president; Cliff C. Stevenson, secretary-treasurer; Earl A. Harris, John E. Felker, A.D. Callison, A.B. Stroud, Robert L. Vogt, and C.O. Garrett. A volunteer auxiliary was formed in 1953 with Doris Larimore as the first president. The hospital continued to expand its facilities and services, and in 1995, it was transferred from the Dominican Sisters of Springfield, Illinois, to the Sisters of Mercy Health System in St. Louis, Missouri.

For the first half of the twentieth century, Rogers's pioneer doctors often worked with the crudest of instruments, mixed their own medicinal powders, made house calls, and, on occasion, accepted bartered items in lieu of cash payments. Their service to the community was commendable. During the celebration of the 50th anniversary of the hospital, these dedicated physicians were honored: Drs. Philo Alden, J.P. Brown, James H. Buckley, Rupert D. Cogswell, William J. Curry, W.C. Edwards, Neal Estes, Guy Hodges, C. Hollow, W.H. Lennox, George M. Love, W.A. McHenry, Clyde McNeil, W.A. Moore, J.C. Pennington, Rufus S. Rice, B.S. Sims, E.N. Stearnes, and C.I. Wheatley.

Business in Rogers continued to flourish through the decades following World War II. One unique company, which produced barrel staves, was begun by E.C. "Lige" Eversole and C.H. Bryant at the end in 1946. White oak trees growing in the Rogers area were first hauled out by horses and then split before going to the mill. The logs were made into staves and sold to various cooperage companies that made whiskey barrels. Only whiskey that has been aged in new, white oak barrels charred on the inside can be called bourbon. Eversole Stave Mill, the last such operating stave mill in Arkansas, closed in 1985.

Another interesting business in Rogers was the Osage Spring Trout Farm, which was formed in 1949 by Clyde Bloomfield for the purpose of bringing fresh trout to the marketplace and also providing a great family place to go fishing. Trout were raised in hatcheries and then put in ponds at maturity. Fishermen of all ages could enjoy casting for trout, and no fishing license was required. Additional ponds were soon dug on land that was once part of Green Valley Farm. Village on the Creeks now covers a portion of the land with upscale shops and restaurants.

Mode O' Day, a women's dress shop, opened in October 1959 at the corner of First and Walnut Streets and then relocated to 110 West Walnut, where it is located today. Still in business over 40 years later, Opal Beck is a strong supporter of business in historic downtown Rogers. Her daughter Sue Fleming shares the retail space with her mother and operates an educational toy and gift business. Opal Beck has an active interest in the history of Rogers and the surrounding area, and she is the primary author and compiler of the book *History of Benton County, Arkansas, Volume I*, published in 1991.

Despite today's competitive world of chain restaurants and fast-food corporations, two of Rogers's downtown businesses that began in the early 1960s are still successful. Owned by J.B. and Patti Head, Susie-Q Malt Shop on Second Street keeps loyal customers lined up at their drive-in except during the colder winter months when they are closed. Hi-D-Ho Drive-In on Walnut Street, owned for many years by Melvin and Joanne Jones and recently purchased by Randy West, keeps hamburgers coming for patrons year round. Many people are still very attracted to a fresh-made burger and personal service.

One nontraditional entrepreneur in Rogers was Tracy Lockhart, a familiar figure on the streets of downtown in the 1930s, 1940s, and 1950s. Tracy was an enterprising peddler whose cheerful call, "Chewing gum, candy, right here handy," often greeted local folks outside the Victory Theater or on the downtown streets. He accepted no charity but earned his living from the creative collection

Tracy Lockhart was a familiar peddler who earned his living in downtown Rogers. He was a welcome sight to patrons attending the Victory Theater. (Sam Wood.)

of items and their sale. He carried his wares in a basket and, later, in a wheelbarrow provided by Beaulieu Hardware.

One of several businesses that have fared well over a long period of time, the Rogers Land Company, founded in 1914 by F.E. Larimore, has promoted Rogers for many years. Harold Roberts, who became a company staff member in 1944, purchased the real estate company in 1957. In 1972, Steve Roberts, Harold's son, joined the company, and in 1974, he became president. Today, the company is affiliated with the Better Homes and Gardens Real Estate national network.

Larger industries also came to Rogers. In 1962, Sam Walton opened the first Wal-Mart Discount store on the corner of Walnut and Eighth Streets, now the site of Shelby Lane Mall owned by Nita Larimore. This giant retail operation started with a successful Ben Franklin franchise store in Newport that was quickly followed by a Walton's 5 & 10 in Bentonville. Wal-Mart, whose headquarters is located in Bentonville, would become the world's leading discount retail operation, dominating the domestic marketplace and taking a leading role in Canada and overseas. Sam Walton's rule to "Exceed your customer's expectations" guided Wal-Mart towards the success it enjoys today. The comprehensive Wal-Mart story is told in the Wal-Mart Museum & Visitors Center on the square in Bentonville.

In a May 1986 edition of *Northwest Arkansas Morning News*, Sam Walton described his view of Wal-Mart's relationship to Rogers, saying, "We will continue to draw upon the people of Rogers and surrounding communities to fill our many associate job opportunities. We also look forward to development of our airport program as we continue to meet our responsibilities to the people of Rogers." His commitment to using the Rogers airport holds true today as a fleet of Wal-Mart Lear jets and a Global Express plane are kept at the airport and used by Wal-Mart employees for business travel. Wal-Mart is also assisting in further expansion, including the construction of a control tower.

Emerson Electric, a manufacturer of unit-bearing appliance motors, opened its plant on Thirteenth Street in Rogers in 1965 and employed over 250 people in the area. As the marketplace changed, the company was forced to close 37 years later. Preformed Line Products Company, which came to Rogers in 1969, makes injection molding and stamping and related products for the telecommunications industry; Swift Chemical Company, which came to Rogers in 1975, manufactures industrial soaps and detergents. Both Glad Home and Automotive Products and Union Carbide began operations in Rogers in 1971; Hudson Foods did the same in 1972; and Scott Paper Non-Woven Products Group in 1973. (A list of other businesses in Rogers can be found at the Rogers-Lowell Chamber of Commerce. Their book of member companies, *Northwest Arkansas Manufacturers and Processors—Benton & Washington Counties*, provides the date a company was formed as well as other pertinent information.)

Wal-Mart opened its very first store under that name on Walnut Street in Rogers in 1962. (Wal-Mart Visitors Center.)

Pauline "Price" Mathias was well loved by her art students at Rogers High School. She was also an active leader of the Blue Demons drill team. (Claudine Haskell.)

Growing up in Rogers in the 1940s and early 1950s was great fun. Television and personal computers had not yet taken over the free time of young people, and organizations in town such as church groups, 4-H, scouts, DeMolays, and Rainbow Girls provided a wealth of activities for children. High school students played sports, marched in the Blue Demons drill team, led the fans as cheerleaders, and belonged to the many clubs offered by the school. One of the favorite hangouts was the Ellis Ice Cream Parlor on Walnut Street that served 27 flavors of ice cream. Jack's Drive on Eighth Street was also a favorite gathering spot of the high-school crowd, and a nickel in the Select-o there would flood the room with hit songs. The skating rink opened at Lake Atalanta in 1948, and a swimming pool, restaurant, and putt-putt golf course were later added. Rogers High School had an open campus, and students could buy their lunches at the Rogers Pharmacy on the corner of Second and Walnut Streets, where Rice Jewelers is today. Students also could pick up lunch or snacks at Rife's store across Walnut Street or from the "little store" on the other side of the high school. "Necking" was popular on the dirt road bordering Lake Atalanta, but young people also enjoyed the drive-in movie theater and two other theatres in town. Twin City Golf, located close to downtown, provided sport for adults.

Teachers had a great influence on the lives of their students, and adults today often compare notes on how one teacher or another pointed them in the right direction. The following teachers are examples of the many who had a positive influence on their students. Pauline "Price" Mathias taught art and science, as well

119

Rogers Mountaineer cheerleaders show their enthusiasm as Steve Roberts bursts through the banner at a Rogers basketball game in the 1950s. The cheerleaders are, from left to right, Sharon Neil, Betsy Bronson, Sheila Jackson, Barbara Kennen, Susan Dubbell, Betsy Robinson, and Dell Christy. (Dell Christy Tyson.)

as sponsored the Blue Demons. Her encouragement is evident in the success of some of her art students, including John Creech and Charles Summey, who both became professional artists. Others found an appreciation for art in her classes that became a source of lifelong satisfaction.

Mary Sue Reagan shared her avid interest in history and politics with her social studies and American history students. She was also a sponsor of the Future Teachers of America club. Betty Lynn Reagan taught history and civics and served as the eighth-grade sponsor. Her dedication to a citizen's rights and responsibilities in our democracy was inspirational. Not all students may have shared their teacher's enthusiasm for history and government while in school, but these teachers set the benchmark by which students would measure their own life's successes. Both teachers, great-great-granddaughters of early mill owner Peter Van Winkle, are still very active in the community and held in the highest esteem.

Florence Edith Robinson was an English and Spanish teacher and sponsored the Spanish Club. One of the things that students remember vividly is her annual reading of Charles Dickens's *A Christmas Carol* to her students. Each year, Tiny Tim's "God bless us every one" brought tears to her eyes. Leith Worthington taught senior English and for many years was elected the senior class sponsor—

an honor that entailed the directing of the annual play. She also sponsored the Press Club and taught journalism and speech. Many of her students who "sat in dread of being called on" in her classroom went on to be English majors in college and published authors. For every student at Rogers High School—regardless of the years—there is a teacher or coach who stands out as having been a positive influence on his or her life.

This dedication in the 1954 *Mountaineer* yearbook demonstrates the special place that the community of Rogers held in the hearts of students:

> We have come to the realization that no school is built in a vacuum. Schools are supported by the surrounding community; they derive much of their color, their character, their traditions from the neighboring countryside. Our lives have been built around Rogers, influenced by its ideals, fashioned by its opportunities for development. There is scarcely a phase of our lives that does not bear its imprint. So to Rogers, a city of homes, schools and churches, a city that has afforded us the best in community living; a city ever mindful of its youth, we dedicate this 1954 *Mountaineer*.

The Ozarks have long been a mecca for creative people. Writers, artists in all mediums, musicians, performers, and crafters have found this area conducive to

High school students sitting on the curb in front of their school building was a familiar sight in the 1950s. (Claudine Haskell.)

their talents. The first craft fair was held in 1954 at War Eagle mill on the old Sylvanus Blackburn farm. Some 40 years later, craft events are still held here in the first weekend in May and the third weekend in October. Joining this rapidly growing industry are shows held throughout Northwest Arkansas at War Eagle Farm, Sharps Show, Quail Oaks, Hillybilly Corner, Ozark Regional, Ole Applegate Place, Ole Applegate Place at the Clarion Hotel, and Dixieland Mall on Walnut Street in Rogers.

According to Vernon Patton, the owner of the Ole Applegate shows, "The combination of individual shows participating in the Northwest Arkansas Craft Show is probably the largest single gathering of crafters in the United States—all within a 20 to 25 mile radius." Jim Inman, the owner and manager of the Dixieland Mall Arts and Crafts Festival in Rogers, says he owes the success of his show to the fresh ideas the crafters bring each year. Hundreds of thousands of craft enthusiasts come to these multiple shows. Many crafters participate in shows around the country as a full-time occupation, while others only show locally once or twice a year. Some husband-and-wife teams double their exposure by simultaneously displaying their crafts at different shows.

Readily available and abundant sources of water have been important to the growth of Rogers since the days of the early settlers. Arkansas ranked sixth among states with the most miles of navigable rivers in the mid-1900s. To provide flood control as well as to create recreational facilities, the Corps of Engineers built

Lake Atalanta was a major recreation facility for families in the 1950s; it boasted a restaurant, swimming pool, skating rink, and boat rentals. (Opal Beck.)

Beaver Dam is under construction in this August 1963 picture taken by the Corps of Engineers. The dam not only supplies abundant water to the area but also draws local families and tourists to the lake for recreation. (U.S. Army Corps of Engineers.)

dams to more effectively channel the Ozark waterways. According to Ben Johnson, author of *Arkansas in Modern America 1930–1999*, "The proliferation of lakes was the most dramatic change in the Arkansas landscape in the second half of the twentieth century."

The White River Basin projects already included Norfolk Lake (built in 1944) and Bull Shoals Lake (built in 1951) before the Beaver Lake project was begun in 1960. To make way for the rising water held by the dam, people were displaced along Beaver Lake shores, and historic sites and cemeteries were moved or covered as the lake filled. "Lost Bridge," near Garfield and Eureka Springs, became permanently lost when the lake filled. Originally built over the White River in 1929, Lost Bridge was, from the start, a bridge going nowhere as access on both sides was not completed for several years due to a lack of funds. People could scramble down a bluff on one side to cross by foot and then climb down a ladder on the other side to complete their crossing. This bridge was eventually washed out in a flood in 1943 and later the lake covered its replacement bridge. Probably the most dramatic site to be flooded was Monte Ne; "Coin" Harvey's dream of a pyramid was lost forever.

The construction of Beaver Dam provided work for people in Rogers and Eureka Springs. These workers stayed on the job from start to finish, and even the roads from the dam site to these two towns were paved so workers could go home at night more easily. The dam, at a length of 2,575 feet, was constructed with 780,000 cubic yards of concrete. Today, Beaver Lake, which has two hydroelectric generators, is the site of both permanent and vacation homes, as well as boating and fishing tournaments. Its scenic beauty draws local residents and tourists alike to this outdoor, recreational area.

The march of history is quite evident in Rogers and Northwest Arkansas. First there was discovery, then settlement and the beginnings of commerce, followed by improvements in community structure and changing types of business enterprises. Inventions, emerging markets, increased and improved education, population growth, and a new awareness of the world obtained through the experience of other cultures during international wars—all affected the small community that grew into the city we know as Rogers today. Wooden sidewalks and buildings in the downtown district were either destroyed by fire or replaced by brick structures to overcome the threat of fire. Schools and churches were built and then torn down, replaced by buildings designed to better meet the needs of the changing times. However, an appreciation for Rogers's unique history inspired community leaders to keep their own stories and structures from fading into oblivion.

Civil War reunions at Pea Ridge began as early as 1887 with both Confederate and Union soldiers participating. Pea Ridge was dedicated as a national military park in 1960, and today, archeologists at the site work to better trace the maneuvers of the battle and to identify and preserve artifacts.

In 1956, Rogers celebrated its 75th anniversary with a celebration organized by executive committee members C.B. Porter, Hardy Croxton, Noel Boulware, John Sample, and Earl Bellmer. Volunteers staffed or chaired 36 committees, and the division chairpeople included Bill Hughes, Doris Larimore, John Walburn, Arthur Deason, C. Jimmie Carter, Ernest Godfrey, Reverend W.L. Miller, and Hardy Croxton. A historical pageant, written and directed by Parker Zellers, presented the history of the town in 16 episodes. The introductory page of the special "Diamond Jubilee" program states the purpose of the celebration quite well.

> The recent progress of Rogers as a City of the First Class in population, industry, agriculture, recreation and civic aggressiveness has brought about a need for a community celebration of such broad scope that it would encompass all of our fellow citizens from all walks of life.
>
> Today each of us knows, understands and appreciates his neighbor better than ever before. This has been our goal from the beginning.

On September 18, 1967, a local crowd gathered to witness the last run of the Frisco's passenger service on the railroad. Though the Frisco station was a distinctive landmark and listed on the National Register of Historic Places in August 1977, it was torn down less than four months later despite a widespread public campaign to save it. Dedicated citizens tried to rescue what they could, including a ticket window and bricks. These artifacts and photographs remind us of the days when the train picked up passengers at the depot, loaded cars with apples and other farm produce, and pulled out of the station. The Frisco Festival held downtown each August continues to celebrate the role the Frisco played in the life of Rogers.

In 1968, the Rogers High School building on Walnut Street was sold and demolished, though in the minds of many former students laughter still fills its halls, students still cram into its locker rooms, and its study hall floor still creaks in tune with footsteps. There is a romance attached to this and many other structures that still resonates with residents today.

Fortunately, Rogers is a community interested in preserving its past as a way to better understand the present and the future. Various groups interested in this kind of civic pride were formed during the 1960s and 1970s and continue today, including the Friends of the Library, the Rogers Art Guild, Daughters of the American Revolution, and the Friends of the Museum. City councilwoman and chairwoman of the bicentennial committee Opal Beck suggested that a worthy project for the bicentennial celebration would be the establishment of a museum in Rogers dedicated to local history. In 1974, Vera Key was appointed to lead this effort and the other coordinators of the project included Peel Strode, Ellen Luffman, Davis Duty, Fred Hiett, Gale Hall, Madeline Lee, Beth Hough, and Marjorie Bryant.

Frank, Lizzie, and Elizabeth Hawkins lived in the home that now houses a portion of the Rogers Historical Museum. (Rogers Historical Museum/Harold Hawkins.)

125

The citizens of Rogers generously donated items from their homes and attics to start the collection for the museum. Space was limited, however, in the leased former First National Bank building on First Street where the museum was initially housed. The first "museum clerks" included Virginia Clark, Ruth Ann Stites, Nancy Mendenhall, and Georgia Hillman, who had the exciting and exacting job of selecting which items would be first placed on display and which items would be held in storage for future programs. Soon, more space was needed to accommodate the growing collection and educational programs. The Friends of the Rogers Historical Museum formally organized in 1976 and set about locating new space.

An ideal space was found, and in 1980 the city purchased the 1895 Hawkins House on Second Street. Improvements were made possible, in part, by donations from Mr. and Mrs. Harold Hawkins's family and a grant from the State of Arkansas Museum Services "disaster" fund. The house museum opened in 1982, and Marianne Woods was hired as the new professionally trained director. She was followed by Jan Harcourt, and then Dr. Gaye Bland, who was hired as director in 1994 and continues to serve in this position. According to Dr. Bland,

> The growth and development of the Rogers Historical Museum since its founding in 1975 has been a real success story. Over the decades the museum moved from leased quarters into its own home, added the 5,600-square-foot Key Wing, and expanded into the former Rogers Public Library building at the corner of Second and Poplar. In the course of these facilities changes, the museum also received numerous state and national awards, garnered many thousands of dollars in state and federal grants, and, in 1999, achieved accreditation by the American Association of Museums. None of this could have been possible without the ongoing support of the City of Rogers, of which the museum is a department. Further, none of this could have been possible without the financial and service support rendered by so many members of this community. The loyalty of museum volunteers in particular is astounding; a number have been regularly volunteering at the museum for two decades!

Major museum exhibits have included "Stitches in Time: A Legacy of Ozark Quilts," "Final Respects: Dealing with Death in the Victorian Era," "The Sagers: Pioneer Cabinetmakers," "Buried Dreams: 'Coin' Harvey & Monte Ne," and "We Did What Had to Be Done: Benton Countians and World War II."

The research library of the Rogers Historical Museum is an excellent resource for the public, containing valuable information about people, events, and organizations pertinent to the history of Rogers. A growing photography file is also part of the research collection, as well as a small library of local and regional history books. The museum staff also prepares informational brochures on many historical topics.

There are, in fact, many wonderful resources for learning about the history of Rogers. The Benton County Historical Society, organized in 1954, began publishing *The Benton County Pioneer,* a periodical filled with stories and historical happenings in the county. J. Dickson Black, a prolific writer of history, penned the *History of Benton County, 1836–1936* in 1975. Countywide newspapers have done exceptional work in preserving the history of the county through their coverage in feature stories and regular columns by writers such as Ruth Muse and Billie Jines. Special editions filled with pictures and stories of the county by staff reporters also serve as excellent educational and research sources.

Thanks to the efforts of countless local people dedicated to preservation, historic downtown Rogers remains the heart of the city and a link to our past, present, and future.

The Vera Key Wing was added to the Rogers Historical Museum in 1987. But the museum is again experiencing growing pains and additional space is needed for the expanding collection and staff. (Marilyn Collins.)

8. A Small Town Grows Up

Small towns in the late 1800s were sometimes left behind and often lost their identity if the railroad was routed elsewhere. In modern times, growth can be stunted if the interstate highway system is located beyond a community. However, Rogers is most fortunate on both these counts. Beginning as a railroad town, Rogers is now, in 2002, experiencing booming economic growth along Interstate 540. In addition, town leaders and citizens whose roots are here—plus those who have chosen Rogers to be their home—embrace the qualities of the past and continue the efforts to preserve it. In an interview with Marilyn Collins in 2001, Mayor Steve Womack appealed to the citizens of Rogers to treasure and preserve their family history and that of the town.

> The best time to start is today, because we can't do it yesterday! Every day real information about the history of Rogers is discarded, lost forever to the community. We can never get it back. We all have family history stored in our attics or basements that, over time, may become forgotten. When we think about the history of Rogers, we first think of the early settlers and town leaders. However, each child born in the city in the year 2001, is also a native of Rogers. Their contributions and stories captured in pictures or print, high school yearbooks, church, and civic activities are our history too. In the future, let it be said that we kept the faith of the past while building a strong and responsible future for our children and our community.

Preservation efforts in historic downtown Rogers helped to create a viable mix of successful retail shops and professional offices, and the juxtaposition of downtown businesses with the later commercial growth on Highway 71 has worked well. Interstate Highway 540, which is slated to become a major south/north connection from southern Louisiana to Kansas City, is emerging as another major corridor of commercial growth along the west side of town. In many places throughout the region, upscale residential communities and commercial developments are replacing the family farm along this growth path. Infrastructure needs, annexation decisions, and quality-of-life issues are under continual review by the appropriate city, county, and state regulating bodies.

Rogers celebrated its centennial in 1981 with speeches, balloons, flags, parades, horse shows, barbershop quartets, outdoor concerts, an auction, and a 100-foot-long cake with the "Frisco train" running its length. Opal Beck served as the chairperson of the centennial committee, which also included members appointed by Jack Cole, the mayor of Rogers at the time: Joye Kelley, Norma Billings, Clarice Moore, Gene Ramsey, Wheeler Litterell, Rick Murphy, Perry Butcher, and Don Law. Centennial Park, which beautified a burned-out space on First Street, was named in honor of the occasion and funded, in part, by Century Club donors and an auction held at the National Guard Armory.

Probably the most spectacular event at the centennial celebration was the logistical success of lifting a caboose, donated by the Frisco railroad and weighing hundreds of tons, from the railroad tracks to a short section of track placed in the Frisco Park just for that purpose. As on the first day the train came to Rogers in 1881, there were plenty of sidewalk supervisors and onlookers as Ken Ewing, with Kan-Ark, used a huge crane to lift and lower the caboose, which is now part of the Rogers Historical Museum.

The *Rogers Daily News* celebrated its 75th anniversary in 1981 as well. The *Rogers Daily Post*, as it was first known, went through various ownerships and eventually morphed into the *Northwest Arkansas Morning News* in 1978. The *Morning News*

The Frisco railroad donated a caboose to Rogers in honor of the Rogers Centennial Celebration. As evident here, it was no easy feat to hoist the caboose off the tracks and on to a section laid for its permanent home in the Frisco Park at the corner of First and Walnut Streets. (Opal Beck.)

published a special 72-page centennial section. This collector's edition represented the culmination of months of labor and was made possible with the help of many local citizens. The newspaper's front page gave special thanks to the Frank A. Mason family, John Applegate, Mrs. Ruth Muse, Max Lough, Pam Dubbell, Dot Summers, Ruth Hurd, the Roy Webster family, and the people of Rogers.

With the impetus of the centennial celebration's focus on preservation, a Main Street project, sponsored by the downtown merchants' association, was undertaken in 1985. Main Street, a program of the National Trust for Historic Preservation, is a national organization dedicated to the preservation and revitalization of downtowns across the country. In 1974, Pots Etc., owned by Barbara Roberts and her partner Jan Barclay, became the first business to move into the then-vacant Vinson Square on First Street. The building's owners, Ernestine Scott and Lorene Stevens, were very supportive of turning the building into a viable commercial location. Following the leadership of Roberts and Barclay, other merchants, including the well-known Crumpet Tea Room, soon filled the space.

In the early 1980s, the downtown merchants' association, led by Roberts, invited Jenny Harmon, who was working on her master's degree in community planning at the University of Arkansas, to speak to the group about her work and the work of the Main Street programs she had witnessed in other communities. Roberts worked to raise public awareness about the Main Street program through newspaper articles, and she presented the request for approval of the project to the mayor and city council. "Rogers was one of the first five cities in the state to apply

Partners Barbara Roberts and Jan Barclay were the first tenants in Vinson Square to make a concerted effort toward revitalization. (Marilyn Collins.)

Dick Trammel of Arvest Bank introduces Main Street director Jenny Harmon at a community-wide event to honor her and Main Street for their leadership in the restoration of downtown Rogers in the 1980s and 1990s. (Rhonda Fleming.)

for acceptance into the program. I was called to Little Rock in September 1984 to receive our approval," said Roberts. "Jenny Harmon was the Main Street director from 1985 to 1999. She had the vision and enthusiasm that helped us see the possibilities of building a strong coalition of business owners, professionals, and those involved in tourism development to invest in our historic downtown." According to John Sampier, mayor from 1981 to 1998, "Rogers was a tailor-made Main Street town. The brick streets anchor the heart of the city. Rogers has a lot of pride and its people like to solve their own challenges."

Maurice Kolman, the director of transportation and planning for the city, and his office worked closely with Harmon. "Jenny was an energetic and delightful person to work with," said Kolman. "She set the tone for downtown redevelopment and the Main Street program in Rogers." The city provided funds to support the Main Street office, and individual property owners handled the cost of restoration, in some cases receiving supplemental grant money. Mike Maloney (president), Sandy Brannan, Opal Beck, Perry Butcher, Marion Bunyard, and Carl Baggett served as the first board of directors for Rogers's Main Street organization. According to Opal Beck, "Old buildings that had fallen into disrepair were in demand and were restored to their original splendor. The domino effect [in reverse] saw building after building repainted, refurbished, and spruced up, inviting people to again shop downtown. Today, if a building becomes empty, it is snapped up almost immediately."

One of the Main Street initiatives was the construction of Frisco Park along First Street in downtown Rogers. A sign in the park lists the organizations participating in the joint project: the United States Department of Transportation (ISTEA), the Arkansas Highway Transportation Department, and local partnerships that included the Downtown Is Uptown Business Association, the Rogers Youth Center Board, the Main Street Rogers Project, the Community

Recycling Center, the Rogers Street Department, the Rogers Water Utilities, the City of Rogers Parks Department, the City of Rogers, and private contributors. Perry Butcher & Associates were the architects, and Midland Construction served as the contractor. The park provides a focal point in downtown for public gatherings as well as an attractive place for families to enjoy.

One of the first investors in downtown restoration during the period of the Main Street project was Sam Fleming. In partnership with Beck Scott and Rex Spivey, he purchased and remodeled the Old Rose Drug Store at 124 West Walnut, today the home of Rice Jewelers and Julie Wait Designs. "We loved the downtown so much and were so happy to have an opportunity to make a difference," said Fleming. "John Sampier, mayor at the time, owned Dean's Men's Wear in a local shopping center. He said if the partnership would make a commitment to downtown, he would move his store downtown—and he did." In the late 1980s, Fleming and Dick Trammel purchased and remodeled the Vance Hill Auto Parts building at 101 West Walnut Street, where Edwards Optical is located today. Fleming, who moved to town in 1976 with his wife, Sue (a native of Rogers), noticed at that time that there were several downtown buildings with boarded-up windows. "We both thought that Rogers was a lovely town and made a commitment, not solely for economic reasons, but because it just needed to be done to help preserve the heart of the city."

Architect and developer H. Collins Haynes of Haynes & Associates Limited has the unique perspective of having developed and restored several downtown buildings and also of being the managing partner of Pinnacle Point I and II, a major new commercial area near I-540 and Champions Drive. In addition to a diverse number of other architectural projects, Haynes first became involved in downtown Rogers in 1982 as the architect for the restoration of the Mutual Aid building on Second and Poplar Streets. Also a managing partner for First Street Holdings, Haynes purchased the Harris Bakery properties on Elm Street and First Street in 1993. "Harris Bakery, constructed in 1936, is still a beautiful building. It is one of the few Art Deco buildings in the state," said Haynes. "They were known as 'America's most beautiful bakery.' " The First Street buildings (built 1888–1890) included in Haynes's purchase were restored and became home to several upscale shops—Iron Horse Coffee Company, Patchwork Emporium, Van Hook Florist & Gifts, Posh Salon, and First Street Art Works. In the parking space used by the Harris Bakery for their bread trucks at 222 First Street, Haynes worked with the Arkansas preservation program to design and construct an "infill" office building on the south side of the Iron Horse Coffee Company. The historic structures on both sides were built on a foundation of stacked rocks; this required that the new building contain 6-foot cantilevered piers to support any pressure from the existing buildings. This new, modern building was deliberately set back from the street to avoid detracting from the streetscape of existing historic buildings. S.C. Johnson Wax, Doane Pet Care, and Edward Jones now share this office space.

The Corner Landing Company, built *c.* 1885 next to the railroad tracks at 117–119 East Walnut, is also a Haynes downtown project. The building, which sat

The completed First Street Plaza (second from left), developed by H. Collins Haynes, includes an infill office building set back from the surrounding buildings to maintain the historic streetscape. (Marilyn Collins.)

on land that belonged to the railroad, was owned as a "use easement" by the Rand Wholesale Company. This ownership arrangement is typical of several properties in Rogers located along the tracks. Railroad cars were once pulled into these side areas, and a ramp connecting the boxcars to the building was used to more easily convey products back and forth. Interestingly, the company had to install a vault to hold revenue stamps that were hand licked and stuck on legally sold cigarette packages. Watson's Bistro once occupied the Corner Landing Company building, which is now home to Vision Technologies, Inc.

The active merchants' association in Rogers eventually grew into the Downtown Is Uptown Merchants Association (DIU), later renamed Historic Downtown Merchant's Association. The organization continues to sponsor retail activities and oversees an aggressive marketing program for the downtown district. "In 1935 . . . what is now called downtown was the hub of the city. Retail stores, banks, professionals, real estate, the post office, automobile dealerships, garages, feed stores, grocery stores, theaters, the Frisco Depot—all were within a cluster of about five city blocks," said downtown merchant Opal Beck. Working cooperatively, DIU, Main Street, the mayor, city council, city departments, and investors interested in restoration have been able to reinvigorate the downtown district with the vitality and commercial success it knew in the early days of the community. Jan Oftedahl, 2001 president of the merchants' association, sees a very different downtown today.

133

The challenges faced by downtown business owners today may be different than in days past, but the respect and gratitude we receive from our customers is the same. We recognize our customers' faces and they recognize ours. People who come into the shops in most cases deal directly with the owner. Downtown is a place where people can still connect one-on-one with each other. Whether it is finding fresh produce at the farmer's market, enjoying live performances at the Victory Theater, strumming and singing with their friends and neighbors at "Pickin' in the Park" on Saturday nights, dining at small restaurants or in a coffee shop, shopping at a wide variety of stores, or touring the museums—downtown is a friendly place to be.

Created in 1998, the Walnut Street Historic District is comprised of a group of commercial buildings originally constructed between 1885 and 1912. While some downtown buildings in Rogers were previously listed on the National Register of Historic Places, the following buildings were included on the 1998 nomination form prepared by Main Street and have since been placed on the National Register:

> Corner Landing Company Building; 117 East Walnut; *c.* 1885; Corner Landing Company, owner
> Rogers Wholesale Grocery Building; 101 East Walnut; *c.* 1907; Dollar Saver, Inc., owner
> Hills Auto Supply Building; 101 West Walnut; *c.* 1888; Charles McCrory, owner
> Walters Building; 103 West Walnut; *c.* 1888; Carl Walters, owner
> Felts Family Shoe Store Building; 105 West Walnut; *c.* 1888; Andy Felts, owner
> Shofner's Building No. 2; 107 West Walnut; *c.* 1888; Jim Shofner, owner
> Shofner's Building No. 1; 109 West Walnut; *c.* 1890; Jim Shofner, owner
> Rogers Hardware Building; 113 West Walnut; *c.* 1898; Charles McCrory, owner
> Southwest Power Company Building; 115 West Walnut; *c.* 1898; Marion Bunyard, owner
> A.D. Callison Building; 117 West Walnut; *c.* 1898; Marion Bunyard, owner
> Elks Lodge Building; 121 West Walnut; *c.* 1909; Paul Parks, owner
> Juhre Building; 202 West Walnut; *c.* 1894; K. Petway, owner
> Union Block Building; 124 West Walnut; 1897; Rex Spivey and Beck Scott, owners
> Stroud Mercantile Building; 114–116 West Walnut; *c.* 1899; Mrs. Harold Wardlaw, owner
> Golden Rule Building, East and West; 110–112 West Walnut; *c.* 1894; Tom Mayfield, owner

Our Place Building; 108 West Walnut; *c.* 1890; Frank Hungerford, owner

Citizens Bank Building; Walnut and First Streets; *c.* 1895; Fred Hunt, owner

Today, Main Street continues to collaborate with downtown property owners on many restoration projects. For example, Emery and Ruth Davis, who own the property on the corner of First and Poplar Streets that once housed, among other businesses, Beaulieu Hardware, are restoring the facade of their building, working with a matching grant of $8,500 from Main Street. Shofner's at 109 West Walnut also underwent a facelift with a $500 matching grant from Main Street.

A particularly unusual preservation effort in town involves Searles Prairie, an undisturbed 10 acres of prairie land located beside Highway 102. Anna Mae Searles donated this conservation easement to the state in 1988. The soil composition and 150 different species of natural grasses and flowers remain here in their natural setting as the only remnant of original prairie protected in the state.

Another historic preservation project begun in the 1990s by Gary Townzen produces an annual calendar filled with historic images of Rogers. The proceeds from this documentary and educational tool benefit the "Feed the Children"

A 2001 Main Street Rogers project is the restoration of the former Beaulieu Hardware building now owned by Emery and Ruth Davis. (Marilyn Collins.)

fund, and Townzen's enthusiasm and knowledge of the history of Rogers help keep the conversation lively in his barbershop on First Street.

Marketing the downtown area, enticing businesses to locate in the historic district, and vigilantly maintaining the historical and structural integrity of downtown buildings continue to be the focus of both the downtown merchants' group and Main Street. Dick Trammel, the executive vice president of Arvest Bank in Rogers and a longtime supporter of downtown revitalization, made the following comment in a 2001 interview with Marilyn Collins:

> People like downtown. Downtown is the center of Rogers. A good mix of retail is possible because money for infrastructure is already in place and doesn't add to the cost of opening a new business. Lower cost of purchase or leasing allows young people and first-time business owners a chance to successfully own their own business.
>
> It's the people downtown that make the difference. They are hard workers, give a lot back to their community, and support the arts, schools, and local churches. As Helen Walton, wife of the late Sam Walton, says, "It is not what we gather in life, but what we scatter in life" that makes the difference.
>
> Rogers people are "can do" folks. Competition, a normal part of the business world, remains outside community projects taken on for the common good. Officers from different banks and a variety of leading business people often serve on the same event and fundraising committees. The philosophy of Arvest bank is reflected in other Rogers' businesses—if we make our community a better place, we will earn our share of the business.

An example of the cooperative efforts of corporate, community, city, and nonprofit groups is the Frisco Festival held each summer since 1985 in downtown Rogers. The commitment of dedicated volunteers, the funding made available by corporate donors and the city, and the involvement of downtown merchants make this event, which is open to the public and free of charge, very successful. Main Street, the sponsoring organization, earmarks proceeds from the festival for worthwhile downtown projects.

Downtown provides a place for the community to come together to enjoy annual events, such as the Homecoming Parade, Goblin Parade, Christmas Parade, Merchants' Holiday Open House, Crazy Days sale, and other activities. In the summer months, people visit the Farmer's Market and gather on Saturday nights in Frisco Park for "Pickin' in the Park," which offers live entertainment. Ben Khone, a bluegrass, gospel, and country music enthusiast, started this annual community event in 1999; it is also open to the public and has no admission charge.

Another important preservation project has been the restoration of the Victory Theater, a Clarke-designed building on Second Street, by the Rogers Little

"Pickin' in the Park" is just one of the many family-oriented activities that takes place in downtown Rogers. Musicians bring their instruments, and small groups gather throughout Frisco Park to enjoy the performances. (Marilyn Collins.)

Theater. The building now provides a beautiful performance space for this group, as well as meeting space for other groups. Bringing the theater back to life has been a continuing community effort. For ten years, the Rogers Little Theater raised money, which they used to purchase the Victory Theater building. Renovation began with a state grant of $36,000, a Main Street Model Business Matching Grant of $25,000, an anonymous gift of $250,000, and a $15,000 grant from the Walton Family Foundation. To date, fundraising efforts have raised $900,000 toward a goal of $2.3 million, and this includes private donations as well as money raised at events sponsored by the theater. Members of the Happy Rackensackers No. 906, part of Questers International (an organization that fosters the preservation and restoration of historical landmarks), provided a $5,000 grant plus funds generated from various events held by their group and contributed a total donation of $15,000 to restore the barrel ceiling in the theater's foyer, one of the most unique architectural features of the building. Other gifts continue to come in. In 2001, the theater foyer was christened "The Strode Foyer" in recognition of a grant from Clarice Moore and her son Matthew Moore. The name honors Clarice Moore's parents, Frank J. and Peel Strode, who owned the Rogers Vinegar Company in the early 1900s.

John Mack, an architect with Perry Butcher and Associates, coordinated the renovation project. According to Joe Mills, "Jim LeFevre, partner in Multi-Craft, was the first to step up and help." He instituted an ice-builder system that the HVAC equipment used to cool the building during peak performance times. This

The Victory Theater (shown during restoration) is a major addition to downtown Rogers, providing the community with an opportunity to perform or to attend live shows throughout the year. (Rogers Little Theater.)

is a less expensive system to install and to run. Mike Jenson, project manager for Nabholz Construction, supervised the engineering and construction contract on the building. Emily and Walter Talbutt served as the managers of the theater from 1934 to 1960, and Emily Talbutt-Patton assisted those working on the renovation by relating firsthand stories of how the theater "used to be."

Luanne Diffin of the Rogers Water Department and Joe Rice of Rice Jewelers led the design committee that was made up of Joe Mills, Simmons First Bank; John Ford, Daisy Museum; Jim Tull, Crafton Tull & Associates; and Jenny Harmon, Main Street. Dr. Gaye Bland, the director of the Rogers Historical Museum, lent her advice and expertise. Joe Mills and Jim Tull continue to lead the fundraising efforts. "Restoration of the theater has been my dream since 1994," remarked Joe Mills. "Many people in Rogers, including me, grew up going to the Victory Theater and I want to see this community tradition maintained. There is nothing like a theater. They're not going to build anything like this anymore. I was the first person to officially step on stage but I've vowed not to perform on this stage until the fundraising goal has been reached."

The Rogers Historical Museum provides a wealth of information about the history of the town and its people. According to Dr. Bland, the museum's five-year plan emphasizes an increasing use of technology to make the museum's collections more accessible to both researchers and museum staff. There are also plans to continue community outreach programs with rotating exhibits at the Rogers Public Library and the Rogers City Administration Building. Dr. Bland also believes that heritage tourism will play an increasing role in the years to come and looks towards the day when the museum can expand to allow space for more exhibits and a growing collection. "As we partner with our neighbors to foster an appreciation of this area's unique heritage, we look forward to continuing to fulfill our mission of serving the community through educating the public about the history and traditions of this area, preserving our local heritage through research and collecting, and providing enriching and enjoyable experiences for all."

Newly opened at 114 South First Street in historic downtown Rogers, the Daisy Airgun Museum provides a detailed history of the Daisy Manufacturing Company that became synonymous with the BB gun in 1888. Former employees of the company who worked at the plant in Michigan and followed Daisy to Rogers join other locally hired employees in volunteering time at the museum and working with the Friends of the Daisy Museum to raise funds for museum programs. A project to preserve the lineage and pedigree of each BB gun that is purchased from the museum provides a "Certificate of Authenticity" to each new owner. A record will be kept in perpetuity of each buyer's name, the series number of their BB gun, the date of its purchase, and any other pertinent information. Other collectible items are offered in numbered, limited editions. While initial funds from Daisy Manufacturing and the City of Rogers helped to get the museum up and running, it is slated to become self-sufficient.

Janet Huckabee, the wife of Governor Mike Huckabee, helped open the new Daisy Airgun Museum on First Street in 1999. Mayor Steve Womack and Perry Butcher welcomed her. (Rhonda French.)

From its meager beginnings with only a few books, the current Rogers Public Library on Dixieland Road now has grown to nearly 90,000 items for loan and research available to the public. According to director Judy Casey, circulation numbers have increased over 100 percent since the library moved to its new location in March 1994. "The library offers a wide number of services to the community," said Casey. "The library is in the process of formulating a five-year strategic plan to meet the changing needs of the community including a changing population. We need to meet the interests of the growing number of professional people, a large increase in Hispanic people and other nationalities to our town, and an influx of retired and elderly population. The populace is more technologically oriented. Over ninety people a day use our computer terminal stations."

"To assist in our funding," continued Casey, "the Friends of the Library is a separate non-profit group that manages the Friendly Book Store of used books on Second Street. Net proceeds from their various efforts including the bookstore are donated to the library each year."

While highway billboards continue to point travelers to historic downtown Rogers, the latest developments off I-540 and in the vicinity of Champions Drive, Horsebarn Road, and Pinnacle Road add a new dimension to the retail and professional energy of Rogers. Village on the Creeks, bordered by Horsebarn Road, Stoneybrook Road, and Osage Creek, offers 275,000 square feet of professional office and upscale retail space. Carmen Lehman of C.R. Lehman Properties has successfully developed this land that was once 21 minnow ponds owned by the Osage Trout Farm.

Located across Osage Creek, where troops once camped during the Civil War, are Pinnacle Point I and II, developed by H. Collins Haynes. This new project

Village on the Creeks is a new upscale retail and professional center with easy access to I-540. (Marilyn Collins.)

St. Mary's Hospital, currently on Walnut Street, is part of the Mercy Health System of St. Louis. Joining the new commercial growth along the I-540 corridor, Mercy Health will be offering additional services to the county in new facilities. (Marilyn Collins.)

offers flexible space to highly mobile corporations seeking amenities usually available only in large urban areas of the United States. The fiber-optic data capability available at the center is unparalleled south of Kansas City. "We're ahead of the curve in Northwest Arkansas and have a tremendous opportunity to do something that's good," said Haynes. "This is a great environment for business. Corporate people relocating here want to leave at first but, after six months, they want to stay and encourage their friends to join them. Quality of life, affordable housing, and amenities to which they are accustomed make them comfortable. They come, they stay, they grow!"

Continuing south is another large project—Pinnacle Hills. A 90-acre upscale development slated to include a $42-million Embassy Suites Hotel and Convention Center developed by John Q. Hammons, Pinnacle Hills is scheduled to open in 2003. Hammons said, "I'm interested in Northwest Arkansas because it is the fastest-growing part of the state and will continue to be in the foreseeable future. Large, growing companies such as Wal-Mart, Tyson, and J.B. Hunt make this area a substantial part of the future economic growth in Arkansas." Currently under construction, Parkway Tower, a part of the Pinnacle Hills Professional Office Complex, will be a six-story, 102,000-square-foot building. When fully completed, the Pinnacle Hills Project is expected to generate $1.2 billion in new construction and to provide more than 40,000 new jobs in the area.

No community can thrive without the support of medical services and a quality hospital. In 1948, the Rice family donated 16 acres of land on which the Rogers Medical Center (which became St. Mary's Hospital in 1979) was built. Since that time the hospital has continued to expand both its services and its space, and off-site medical centers have provided more convenience to residents in the area. In

1997–1998, the Mercy Health System of St. Louis consolidated health care in Benton County, forming the Mercy Health System of Northwest Arkansas, and in 1998, Susan Barrett became the chief executive officer and president of this countywide program. Donated by the late Evelyn Rife and family, a 75-acre tract of land, located to the east of I-540 and south of New Hope Road, will be the new home of Mercy Hospital's medical services campus and was in the preliminary planning stages in late 2001. The Mercy project is part of an overall cooperative project with Great Northwest Development Company for the site. "The gift was a true blessing to Mercy and will be a tremendous benefit to this region," said Barrett. "I also want to acknowledge Pete Walsh and his family for their gift of land that makes it possible for us to plan the entire property for its highest and best use."

New Hope Road will be widened through the old Rife farm, though the exact location is still under consideration at this writing. On the south side of Pinnacle Hills Parkway, Perry Road will be widened from Champions Drive to the new Rogers High School, which opened in 2001. Other road improvements that will be completed in several sections are planned from Highway 71 Business to beyond Pleasant Grove Road.

Rogers has, for the most part, stayed ahead of the curve in providing the necessary infrastructure for the community's projected development. Work by the various departments of the city is essential for the smooth operation the city, and the list of current departments reflects the changes and growth that the city is experiencing. These departments include the following: Office of the Mayor, City Attorney, City Clerk, Code Compliance, Treasurer, Transportation and Planning, Fire Department, Municipal Court Judge and Clerk, Police Department, Water Department, Airport Manager, Building Inspector, Cemetery, Library, Rogers Historical Museum, Parks Department, Rogers Youth Center, and Street Department.

The new home of the Rogers Police Department on New Hope Road and Dixieland Road opened in 1999. These facilities helped provide the Rogers Police Department with the expansion room they needed in order to meet the growing concerns of citizens. Chief Tim Keck has initiated new programs to meet the evolving nature of crime in the area and to ensure that officers receive the training and internal counseling support required to be as effective as possible.

In 2000, Walnut Street was widened from downtown Rogers to I-540, energizing new business along its path. The Scottsdale Center includes Kohl's Department Store and the multiplex Malco's Cinema. Office Depot, Lowe's, Hampton Inn, numerous restaurants, and smaller, newly built retail shops now surround this intersection. A number of other new businesses are joining this retail area, including Pier 1, Belk, Linens and Things, Gap, and Old Navy. Planned, quality business growth is important to the city, and this is a belief that Mayor Steve Womack expressed in his "State of the City" address in January 2001. "Clearly, the massive growth of the commercial and retail sector has the greatest potential impact on our city. No one can discount the importance of improving our business trade. Since half of our total city revenue comes in the form of sales tax collections, it should be obvious that attracting more shoppers to our community enhances our ability to serve our citizens."

The Rogers airport is keeping up with the times also. In 2001, a new runway was laid, providing a surface capable of handling larger planes, and Wal-Mart Aviation, which calls Rogers Municipal Airport/Carter Field home, is in the process of a multi-million-dollar expansion project there. The involvement of Wal-Mart at the airport (in addition to the airport's position as a hub for business travel in Northwest Arkansas) has allowed the airport to function independently from the general city fund. The airport offers charter service, flight training, repairs, fuel, air ambulance service, and rental cars. Private planes are also hangared there. Maurice Kolman, the planning director for the city, boasted, "The airport in Rogers is the finest all-weather, general aviation airport in Northwest Arkansas."

In 1994, through the efforts of many people including Don Tyson, J.B. Hunt, and the family of the late Sam Walton, federal funds were made available to purchase land for the Northwest Arkansas Regional Airport (XNA) located 15 miles west of Rogers. The Northwest Arkansas Regional Airport Authority held its first meeting in 1990, and representatives of the governments of Rogers, Bentonville, Fayetteville, Siloam Springs, and Springdale, as well as those of

Northwest Arkansas Regional Airport opened in 1998, and President Bill Clinton presided over the dedication service. Accompanying him on the platform are, from left to right, Rodney Slater, secretary of transportation; Steve Green, chairman of the Airport Authority; U.S. Senator Tim Hutchinson; Jane Garvey, administrator of the Federal Aviation Administration; and U.S. Congressman Asa Hutchinson. (Northwest Arkansas Regional Airport.)

Benton and Washington Counties, made up the council. The new facility was dedicated on November 6, 1998, with American Eagle, American Airlines, ASA Delta Connection, Northwest, Trans World Express, and US Air carriers providing service to nine destinations. According to executive director and chief executive officer Scott Van Laningham, XNA in 2001 was running two to three years ahead of projections. The airport provides the opportunity for heavy corporate travel with over 40 flights available per day. Plans for expansion are already in the making to stay the course with increased development in Northwest Arkansas.

The availability of quality housing and recreation choices also plays an important role in attracting people to the area. Charles Reaves of C.R. Reaves FLP is developing Shadow Valley, a master planned community southwest and west of Pinnacle and bordered on the west by Highway 112 and on the east by South Rainbow Road. These 514 acres will include a gated community of 850 to 1,000 houses, walking/jogging trails, pocket parks, a soccer field, a swimming pool, a clubhouse, and other amenities. Two hundred acres will be devoted to an 18-hole golf course. Reaves came to Northwest Arkansas as a child and thought it a beautiful part of the country. As an adult, he still feels the same about the area. "The economic conditions are really good and I feel that they will be that way for quite some time. It is the area that attracts people. People coming here are not as tied to individual towns. As the towns grow closer together, the borders become less discernable."

Members of the Rogers Advertising and Promotions Committee work with chamber of commerce staff to handle the use of a 2-percent room tax collected by hotels/motels for the purpose of drawing more people to Rogers with plans including an overnight stay. According to chamber president Raymond Burns,

> It is a natural extension from dollars spent for lodging to dollars spent for retail products, in restaurants, and for local recreation. We need to offer more entertainment opportunities for families living here now and to attract new families in the future. One popular recreational opportunity sponsored by the Rogers-Lowell Area Chamber of Commerce is the Buddy Bass Fishing Tournament held each year. The 2001 tournament drew 800 participants with 400 boats to Beaver Lake, and prizes, totaling around $35,000, included a fully rigged bass boat, motor, and trailer.
>
> Jobs in the years to come will be driven by emerging technology. Jobs available 10 to 20 years from now have not even been thought of yet. People who take these jobs will embrace change. They will work hard and want to also play hard. Discussions are underway now to determine the best approach to meet future recreation and leisure time needs.

The chamber of commerce serves business interests by focusing on the best means of continued economic development in the area. "People here wouldn't

The Rogers-Lowell Chamber of Commerce supports strong, planned business growth. Part of this service is helping to build effective business people through its Leadership Rogers Program. Above is the first Leadership Rogers class. (Rhonda French.)

even think of not working together," said Burns. "The more we do together, the more we will achieve." The Chamber's Leadership Rogers-Lowell Program brings 20 businesspeople together in a new class each year to learn more about the area and develop ideas for improvement. First Leadership, a program sponsored by Arvest/First National Bank and geared to high school sophomores and juniors with a grade-point average of 3.0 or better, enrolls 15 to 20 students from September through May. This program helps students develop their leadership skills as they learn more about the community, its history, government, arts, and business enterprises.

As 2001 comes to a close, the era of prosperity and growth continues in Northwest Arkansas and the City of Rogers. Rogers is uniquely situated with I-540 at its border, abundant water, planned infrastructure in place, and forward-looking, positive-minded leaders and business people prepared to develop the best and wisest use of the available opportunities. Churches and schools continue to expand and adapt to today's emerging expectations and needs.

Reverend Ben Rowell, the recently retired pastor of the First Baptist Church after 26 years, says that local churches are also responding to the changing needs of people in the area. Contemporary programs, held in many churches, offer more music (often enhanced with live instrumental accompaniment) and shorter sermons, and some churches also offer second-language services. "Churches are in transition with the greatest growth in the more contemporary churches," stated Rowell. Continued interest in the church is clearly reflected in the number of satellite missions underway around the city.

Dr. Janie Darr, the superintendent of Rogers public schools, believes that there will continue to be "growth over the next ten years and the need for new schools will depend on the age distribution of students." Wide community support for the schools is evidenced by the number of schools and special buildings named for local people who have had a profound effect on education in Rogers. School names are selected by the board of education and include the following: Bonnie Grimes Elementary, J.W. Grimes Vocational Building, Grace Hill Elementary, Leith Worthington Auditorium, Mary Sue Reagan and Betty Lynn Reagan Elementary, (David) Gates Stadium, Russell D. Jones Elementary, Dorothy Ross Building, Frank Tillery Elementary, W.E. King Gymnasium, Joe Mathias Elementary, Greer Lingle Middle School, and Birch Kirksey Middle School. Rogers's schools also honor athletes and strong supporters of athletic programs with induction into the Mountie Hall of Fame. To date, the following people have been selected for this distinction: Dr. Bill King, Larry Melson, Howard Sutton, Reverend Ben Rowell, Whitie Smith, Frank Tillery, Blackie Bond, Fred Summers, Jerry Ferguson, Steve Roberts, and Dale Bland.

A school system flourishes with community support and dedicated educators. Dr. Janie Darr, superintendent of schools, shares the system's pride in these individuals, for whom a school or facility has been named. From left to right are (front row) Dr. Darr, Mary Sue Reagan, Betty Lynn Reagan, Russell D. Jones, and Grace Hill; (back row) David Gates, Bonnie and Bill Grimes, Frank Tillery, and former superintendent Dr. Roland Smith. (Philip Martin & Lifetouch.)

Rogers and the surrounding area are experiencing a significant change in the demographics of the population. The 2000 census lists a total population in Benton County of 153,406 people, and a breakdown of this total shows the following racial makeup in the county: 139,399 Caucasian; 629 black or African American; 2,531 American Indian and Alaska Native; 1,673 Asian; 130 Native Hawaiian and other Pacific Islander; 13,469 Hispanic or Latino (of any race); and 2,791 of two or more races. Projected population growth for Benton County over the next ten years brings the total number of residents to an estimated 250,000 people. An increasing number of retired persons are finding Benton County to be an ideal haven, and as in the 1970s, when Rogers experienced an influx of new Vietnamese residents, the 1980s saw the beginning of a still-growing Hispanic community in the area.

In Rogers, the Hispanic population of 7,490 makes up a little more than 19 percent of the total Rogers population of 38,829. To meet the demands that these changing demographics require, Mayor Steve Womack and the Rogers City Council established the Rogers Community Support Center in 2000 to "promote, educate, and serve the diverse cultural interests of Rogers, uniting the community as one." The board of directors reflects the broad community support for this service and includes the following members: Marilyn Barnes, Arvest Bank; Emma Cardozo, Wal-Mart; Molly Hunt, Ro-Ark; Steve Carter, Ro-Ark; Ida Fineberg, Lindsey & Associates; Greg Graham, Poplar House; David Bugea, Arvest Bank; Lorena White, Peterson Farms; Exell LaFayaette, Wal-Mart; Tamara Burnett, Tyson Foods; and Fairy Degener, student at Northwest Arkansas Community College. The Support Center is directed by Cesar Aguilar. "This community has a can-do attitude," said Cesar Aguilar. "Financial support has come from the Walton Family Foundation, Arvest Bank, First Christian Church, City of Rogers, and the Rogers-Lowell Chamber of Commerce. Building awareness and understanding of each other, regardless of national origin, is our main focus."

Rogers was one of the first cities to incorporate recreation for young people through the sharing of space, materials, and personnel between the schools and the city's youth center. Under this system, the cost of building duplicate gyms and other facilities is eliminated. Originally, Gene Foerster bought 5 acres of land and began the construction of a center for children's activities. He got the job started, and then the community stepped in to complete the project on the land Foerster deeded to the city. The 24,000-square-foot youth center building was completed in 1982 and constructed with no tax dollars. According to Foerster, it serves citizens from ages "1 to 101."

A new building, slated to open in June 2002, is currently under construction and will expand the space to over 56,000 square feet. The Walton Family Foundation donated $2.3 million for construction, but another $2 million is needed to complete the center with furnishings, equipment, landscaping, signage, and an outdoor park. The outdoor area will include a skateboard park, splash park, and a challenge climb. (Rogers youth have already raised $16,000 for the skateboard park.) The new building will contain three gyms, a computer lab with

East Elevation

Another way the community shows pride in its youth is the very busy Rogers Youth Center. A new building is now under construction; this is the east elevation of the new center. (Rogers Parks and Recreation.)

25 computers, a study lab with a certified teacher, four additional classrooms, and a photo lab. According to Director Jim Welch, "We wore off the front door of the old center—hinges and all—four times since 1982." The primary focus of the center is children, but activities for senior citizens will also continue there until a Senior Community Center can be funded and built. In 2001, about 1,200 children (4,000 during peak periods) use the center on a daily basis for programmed activities. In addition, another 150 kids drop in after school each day and stay until their parents finish work. The new center will have room for an additional 450 youngsters for the drop-in program.

From its beginning in 1881 through today, Rogers has been home to energetic and community-minded people. Although the world seems to have suddenly changed around us, that spirit still prevails. On September 11, 2001, an unprecedented act of terrorism was carried out on the New York City World Trade Center and the Pentagon in Washington, D.C., and Americans have again been called upon to support a national and international effort to fight the enemy. Men and women of Rogers have been asked to serve our country, including Rogers mayor Steve Womack, commander of the 2nd Battalion, 153rd Infantry Regiment of the 39th Separate Infantry Brigade of the U.S. Army National Guard, who was deployed in October 2001 to the Middle East.

A memorial service following the terrorist attacks on September 11, 2001, was held by the Rogers Fire and Police Departments to honor the men and women who lost their lives at the World Trade Center and the firefighters and police who labored to save them. At the service, Wendy Shumate, assistant to the mayor, read the following excerpts from the letter Mayor Steve Womack sent to Pastor David Hadsell, the chaplain serving both departments:

We all remain in a state of shock following the tragic events of September the 11th. Words cannot express the deep sense of loss for all Americans and profound sorrow we have for those victimized. Images of airliners disappearing into buildings, innocent civilians leaping to certain death, and skyscrapers tumbling into a pile of rubble will forever remind us of this awful human tragedy. Let us also remember the inherent dangers faced every day by the men and women who proudly wear the uniforms of police officers, firefighters, and search and rescue personnel. They, like those in our armed forces, are the pride of America! I wish I could be with you on this occasion; however, military activities at Fort Leavenworth, Kansas, kept me away. God bless you all and God bless America.

As we close this chapter on the City of Rogers, the story continues. We preserve what is good from our past and, as a community, build what is best for our future. Officially, the town began with the advent of the railroad and grew as apples, peaches, strawberries, and, later, chickens filled its cars. Churches and schools flourished, shops sprang up along the tracks, and roads leading in and out of the city were built. The source of our economy changed over the years and will surely change in the future. Whatever tomorrow holds, the town of Rogers and this community of people are prepared to successfully meet the challenges ahead.

American flags flew proudly from buildings and along the streets in support of our country and to commemorate the thousands who died in the September 11, 2001, terrorist attacks. (Marilyn Collins.)

Appendix I
A Timeline of Rogers History

1541   Hernando de Soto crosses the Mississippi, becoming the first recorded white man
       in Arkansas

1682   Arkansas becomes the formal possession of France

1721   John Law settles at Arkansas Post, later the county seat of Arkansas County

1776   Revolutionary War occurs and independence is won from Great Britain

1783   At the end of the war, the Treaty of Paris gives America the east bank of the
       Mississippi River

1799   Spanish census records 368 people in Arkansas District

1803   The Louisiana Purchase includes 828,000 square miles, encompassing the future
       Benton County

1806   District of Arkansas is designated

1810   First U.S. census records population of 1,062 in Arkansas

1811   New Madrid earthquake occurs

1813   Arkansas County is created by the Missouri territorial legislature

1816   William Lovely purchases land including what is today Northwest Arkansas

1819   Congress creates the Territory of Arkansas and the first territorial legislature meets
       at Arkansas Post

1820   Arkansas population is 14,273

1821   Territorial capital moves to Little Rock

1828   Adam Batie is the first white settler in Benton County, settling near Maysville
       Cherokee Indians exchange their Arkansas lands for land farther west into
       designated Indian Territory
       Washington County, which includes the future Benton County, is established

1830   Census records 30,388 people in Arkansas

1830s Jacob Roller from Tennessee settles on Roller's Ridge near Garfield
       William Reddick and Samuel Burks from Illinois settle near Elkhorn

1832   Issac and Levi Borne are the first white settlers on the War Eagle Creek

1836   Arkansas enters the Union as the 25th state and a slave state
       Benton County is organized and Bentonville is designated the county seat the
       following year

1830s "Trail of Tears" comes through Northwest Arkansas

1839   First school in Benton County opens in the Masonic Lodge at War Eagle

1840   Arkansas population is 97,574; Benton County, 2,228

1846   War with Mexico begins; Benton County men enlist at Fort Smith

1849   First parties lead the gold rush from Fort Smith to California

1851   Peter Van Winkle and family move to Benton County and construct a sawmill at War Eagle

1858   Butterfield Overland Stage stops at Callahan's Tavern

1860   Arkansas population 435,450; Benton County, 9,285

1861   Arkansas secedes from the Union, joins the Confederacy

Arkansas troops take part in Confederate victory at Oak Hills, also named Wilson's Creek, near Springfield, Missouri

1862   Confederates lose at the Battle of Pea Ridge, also called Battle at Elkhorn Tavern

1865   Robert E. Lee surrenders to General Ulysses S. Grant

President Lincoln is assassinated

Post Colonies (camps) were set up to protect women and children in Benton, Washington, and Madison Counties

1866   Congress establishes military law in Arkansas

1868   H.B. Horsley settles near Rogers and, later, builds the Electric Springs Hotel

Arkansas is readmitted into the Union under Reconstruction

1870   Arkansas population is 484,471; Benton County is 13,831

1873   B.F. Sikes returns to Rogers. He offers land in Rogers to the St. Louis & San Francisco Railroad; other Rogers businessmen also put up money when the railroad begins surveying in 1880.

1881   First passenger train comes to Rogers on May 10

Town of Rogers incorporates on May 28

Rogers Champion, first newspaper, is published

New Era, second newspaper, is published a few days later

John P. Hely surveys first 15 blocks of Rogers for B.F. Sikes

Congregational Church is first established church in the new town

1883   First bank, Bank of Rogers, is established by W.R. Felker

International Order of the Odd Fellows organizes in Rogers

Rogers Academy is established

1884   Arkansas apples win first prize at New Orleans Exposition

Stroud's opens and remains in operation until 1993

1886   Fire destroys many downtown buildings in Rogers

1887   First Masonic Lodge organizes in Rogers

First reunion of veterans of the Battle of Pea Ridge is held

1888   First telephone lines run in Rogers, and first waterworks system is established

Rogers Hose Company organizes

First Benton County Fair is held in Rogers

1890   Arkansas population is 1,128,211

1891   Arkansas' first "Jim Crow Law," the Separate Coach Bill, is signed into law

Poll Tax becomes the prerequisite for voting

1893   First hospital is established in Rogers

1895 William Jennings Bryan, 1896 Democratic Presidential nominee, speaks at the local Chautauqua

First electric lights are installed in downtown Rogers

1896 Opera House opens over W.A. Miller store

First officially held football game pits Rogers against Bentonville

1897 First motion picture is shown at the Opera House

Mas Luz Club forms

1898 Arkansas sends two regiments to the War with Spain

Harvey Dining Hall opens in Rogers

Rogers Telephone Office opens

1899 Arkansas Industrial University changes name to the University of Arkansas

1900 W.H. "Coin" Harvey establishes Monte Ne resort

1901 Apple blossom becomes Arkansas State emblem

1902 Bank of Rogers installs the first adding machine in Rogers

Rogers Transfer and Storage opens

Mas Luz Club changes its name to the Women's Study Club

Governor Jeff Davis speaks at the Opera House

1903 Rogers becomes a Second Class city by special census records; Rogers population is 2,563

Rogers businessmen unsuccessfully try to change county seat to Rogers

Rural Free Delivery begins

First concrete sidewalks are built in downtown

1904 A.O. Clarke, architect, moves to Rogers

First public library opens in town

First bridge is built over the White River in Benton County

1905 O.L. Gregory builds the first vinegar plant in northwest Arkansas; it becomes the largest in the world

Kruse gold mine starts operation in Rogers

Rogers Wholesale Grocery is incorporated

1906 Carrie Nation comes to Rogers

1907 Yellow Fever epidemic sweeps the country, including Rogers

D.A.R. forms in Rogers

Mutual Aid Union insurance company opens in Rogers

1908 Leander Norris is elected county judge as the first Republican to be elected to county office since the Civil War

Will Rogers marries Betty Blake at her home on 307 East Walnut Street

1909 Tom McNeil opens the first auto dealership in the county

First sewer system contract is let to Riley Construction

1910 Benton County Extension Service is started

First movie theater opens

Rogers Daily Post begins publication

1911 First city mail delivery begins

Elks Lodge #1223 organizes in Rogers

Original Rogers High School is built and opened

1912   Children's Aid Society of New York City brings orphans by train with a stop in
            Rogers—known as the "Orphan Train"
        First Boy Scout troop organizes in Rogers
1913   Father Bandini from Tontitown dedicates first Catholic Church in Rogers
1914   New brick railroad depot is built south of Cherry Street
        Interurban rail line opens between Rogers and Bentonville
        Campus Park, first park in town, is landscaped on Rogers Academy campus
        Rogers Academy is closed; property is transferred to the Rogers School District
1915   Typhoid fever epidemic rages and Rogers institutes water treatment for city water
1916   Rogers High School is granted accreditation by the Southern Association of
            Colleges and Secondary Schools
        Statewide prohibition begins
1917   America enters World War I on April 6
        Rotary Club organizes in Rogers
1918   World War I ends
        Worldwide influenza epidemic hits Rogers
1919   Women are granted full suffrage by the Nineteenth Amendment
1920   Benton County population is 36,253; Rogers is 3,318
1921   First commercial broilers are raised in Benton County
1923   First Apple Blossom Festival is planned in Rogers; Ruby Robinson is voted queen
        Kiwanis Club organizes in Rogers
        First radio station, KUOA, opens in Rogers
1925   Arkansas becomes the first state to ratify the Child Labor Amendment
        T.E. Harris family takes over management of the American National Bank, later
            named the First National Bank
1927   Great flood covers one-fifth of Arkansas land
        Victory Theater opens
        Last Apple Blossom Festival in Rogers occurs
        First 4-H Club organizes in town
1928   Teaching of evolution is banned in public schools
        Jim Shofner purchases *Rogers Daily Post*, changes name to *Rogers Daily News*
1929   Lane Hotel opens
        First sound movies are shown at the Victory Theater
        Stock market crashes on Wall Street on October 29
        Louise Thaden, woman pioneer aviatrix from Bentonville, wins the All Women's
            Air Derby and is later included in Smithsonian Institution Aviation Hall of Fame
        Vera Key organizes Rogers Garden Club
1930   Highway 71 is built between Rogers and Bentonville
        Arkansas population, 1,854,482; Benton County, 35,258; Rogers, 3,554
1931   Rogers library opens on second floor of City Hall
1932   "Coin" Harvey unsuccessfully runs for President on the Liberty Party ticket
        First Girl Scout troop in county organizes in Rogers
1933   Prohibition is repealed
1934   Tyson Foods and House of Webster are founded

1935   Improvements in milk production lead to Pet and Carnation Milk companies locating plants in Rogers

Harris Baking Company opens in Rogers

Will Rogers is killed in an airplane crash

1936   Lake Atalanta is built as a WPA project

1938   Burns Funeral Home opens in Rogers

1940   First draft registration occurs on October 16

Arkansas population is 1,949,387; Benton County is 36,148; Rogers is 3,550

1941   Japan attacks Pearl Harbor

National Guard Armory is built on Eighth Street in Rogers

1942   Last Union veteran in Rogers, "Uncle Benny" Martin, dies at 100 years of age

1943   Tyson Company purchases its first farm

1945   Rogers Airport Association is organized

World War II ends

1947   Munsingwear hosiery plant opens in Rogers

Rogers become a "City of the First Class"

Rogers airport begins to receive shipments of baby chicks

1948   Hastings Hatchery, largest in the world, builds in Rogers

1950   Korean War begins June 25

Arkansas population is 1,909,511; Benton County is, 38,076; Rogers is 5, 222

1951   Sisters of St. Dominic become managers of Rogers Memorial Hospital/St. Mary's

Pel-Freez opens in Rogers

1953   Arkansas is designated "The Land of Opportunity"

1954   U.S. Supreme Court invalidates school segregation

First craft fair is held at War Eagle by the Northwest Arkansas Handweavers Guild

Rogers Tool Works opens in Rogers

Benton County Historical Society organizes

1956   Rogers holds Diamond Jubilee Celebration

Television comes to Northwest Arkansas

1957   Arkansas National Guard is ordered to Little Rock's Central High School by Governor Faubus to prevent integration

1958   Daisy Manufacturing moves to Rogers

1960   Work begins on Beaver Dam by Army Corps of Engineers

Contract is let for new Rogers Post Office; former post office on Poplar Street becomes Rogers-Hough Memorial Library in honor of Cass Hough

Major fire occurs on First Street

Pea Ridge National Military Park is dedicated

1962   Wal-Mart #1 opens in a 16,000-square-foot store in Rogers

1964   Constitutional amendment eliminates poll tax

Arkansas ranks second in the nation for broiler and turkey products

1966   Beaver Dam is completed

Winthrop Rockefeller is elected the first Republican governor since Reconstruction

1967   Last passenger train leaves Rogers

1969 State buys the Roscoe Hobbs estate in Rogers as a wildlife refuge

1970 Arkansas population is 1,923,295; Benton County is 50,476; Rogers is 11,050
      Poet Edsel Ford, former Rogers High School student, dies

1972 Hudson Foods opens in Rogers
      Lindsey & Associates is founded in Rogers
      Buffalo National River bill is signed
      Rogers Art Guild is formed

1975 Rogers Historical Museum opens on First Street in the former Bank of Rogers
           building
      Walton family purchases First National Bank

1976 Rogers celebrates U.S. bicentennial with reenactment at Pea Ridge Military Park

1978 Rogers Recycling Center opens, run by volunteers
      William Jefferson Clinton is elected governor of Arkansas
      Major fire occurs in downtown

1980 Dixieland Mall opens

1981 Rogers Centennial Celebration is held in Rogers

1982 Burlington Northern purchases the Frisco railroad
      Rogers Historical Museum moves to South Second Street

1984 Rogers is designated a Main Street city

1987 Governor Bill Clinton declares Arkansas "The Natural State," General Assembly
           never officially approves the slogan

1988 Block on Walnut Street is placed on the National Register of Historical Places

1989 Belgium-owned Bekaert tire-cord company opens in Rogers
      Tyson Foods purchases Holly Farms and becomes world's largest integrated
           poultry business

1990 Bill Clinton is elected to fifth term as governor of Arkansas
      Arkansas population is 2,350,725; Benton County is 97,499; Rogers is 24,367
      Northwest Arkansas Community College begins its first term of classes

1991 Bond issue is approved for a new library to be built on Dixieland Road
      The local National Guard unit under Captain Gregory Watkins is deployed to
           Dhahran, Saudi Arabia as part of Desert Shield/Desert Storm

1992 Bill Clinton is elected President of the United States
      Former President George Bush awards Sam Walton "Medal of Freedom"

1998 Northwest Arkansas Regional Airport (XNA) is dedicated by President Clinton

1999 Rogers Historical Museum receives accreditation
      New Rogers Police Department building is dedicated
      Daisy Airgun Museum opens
      Advertising & Promotion Commission organizes to promote tourism/business
      Interstate 540 is completed from Benton County to Interstate 40

2000 Rogers Youth Center receives grant from the Walton Family Foundation
      Tyson Foods celebrates its 65th anniversary

2001 New Rogers High School opens

Appendix II
Town Leaders

Mayors

1881	J. Wade Sikes	1912–1913	W.F. May
1882	A.J. Allen	1914–1915	J.O. Jones
1883	W.H. McFarlin	1916–1917	W.F. May
1884	A.J. Allen	1918–1919	H.U. Funk
1885–1886	J.B. Steele	1920–1922	H.U. Funk
1887	J.P. Woolsey	1922–1927	H.T. Penn
1888	J.B. Steele	1928–1929	J.H. Rood
1889	E.R. Morgan	1930–1931	Dr. T.E. Hodges
1890	J.B. Steele	1932–1943	F. W. Vinson
1891–1894	H.M. Frazier	1944–1947	J. Frank Smith
1895–1896	T.J. Keller	1947–1953	R.L. Vogt
1897	E.R. Adamson	1954–1955	J. Frank Smith
1898	W.A. Miller	1956–1959	Harold Roberts
1899–1900	E.R. Morgan	1960–1963	W. Seward Puckett
1901–1902	R.L. Nance	1964–1974	Ed Bautts
1903	R.P. Owens	1975–1978	Harry B. Smith
1903–1905	R.L. Nance	1979–1981	Jack Cole
1906–1907	Jay Dalton	1981	John Sampier (acting mayor)
1908–1909	E.W. Homan		
1910–1911	W.F. May	1982–1998	John Sampier
1912	W.F. Rozelle	1998–present	Steve Womack

CITY MARSHALS

1881–1886	Robert Sikes
1887	C. W. Vandegriff
1888–1892	H. Hornback
1893–1902	J.J. Barnett
1903–1905	Cash Parker
1906–1907	J.L. Shinpaugh
1908–1909	James Hardin
1910–1911	John Shinpaugh
1912–1913	J.B. Atkinson
1914–1917	Frank Vinson
1918–1920	J.B. Atkinson
1903–1905	Cash Parker
1906–1907	J.L. Shinpaugh
1908–1909	James Hardin
1910–1911	John Shinpaugh
1912–1913	J.B. Atkinson
1914–1917	Frank Vinson
1918–1920	J.B. Atkinson
1921	T.C. McSpadden
1922–1926	J.H. Roper
1926–1929	J.T. Carroll
1932–1935	O.C. Roller
1936–1942	Walter Reddick
1942–1944	W.C. Dean

POLICE CHIEFS

1944–1953	W.C. Dean
1953–1962	Quant Morrison
1962–1964	Joe Means
1965–1970	Carlton Brown
1971–1977	Jack Cole
1976–1977	Jimmy B. Luster
1977–1980	Charles Gourley, Jr.
Jan–Apr 1978	Dennis H. Musteen (acting chief)
1980–1992	Dennis H. Musteen
Nov 1980–May 1981	Charles Gourley Jr. (acting chief)
1992–1999	Charles M. Jones
1999–present	Tim D. Keck

FIRE CHIEFS (ROGERS HOSE COMPANY)

1888–1889	John H. Rebholtz
1889–1892	J.W. Frey
1892–1894	W.D. Baker
1894–1896	Arthur Miller
1896–1898	J.A.C. Blackburn
1898–1899	Dick Huskins
1899–1900	Arthur Miller
1900–1902	J.M. Derreberry
1902–1903	C.O. Short
1903–1905	Hugh Puckett
1905–1906	J.C. McSpadden
1906–1910	Finis Miller
1910–1912	Berry Walker
1912–1914	Frank Owens
1914–1919	Arch Owens

FIRE CHIEFS (ROGERS FIRE DEPARTMENT)

1919–1922	Ora Noakes
1922–1953	Dr. George M. Love
1953–1966	Frank Jacobs (acting chief, 1950–1953)
1966–1976	Richard Graves
1976–1981	Robert Whitley
1982–1999	Kenneth Riley
1999–2002	Rick Williams
2002–present	Wesley Lewis (acting chief)

SCHOOL SUPERINTENDENTS

1908–1912	A.B. Mayberry
1912–1913	no superintendent
1913–1916	Fred Angwin
1916–	M.O. Alcorn
–1922	James W. Oliver
1922–	Charles Baldwin
–1932	Dale Morrison
1932–1955	Birch L. Kirksey
1955–1983	Greer Lingle
1983–1993	Frank Tillery
1993–1999	Roland Smith
1999–present	Janie Darr

Selected Bibliography

Allsopp, Fred W. *Folklore of Romantic Arkansas*, Vol. 1. New York: The Grolier Society, 1931.

Benton County Heritage Committee. Opal Beck, ed. *History of Benton County, Arkansas*. Dallas: Curtis Media Corporation, 1991.

Benton County Historical Society. *Goodspeed's 1889 History of Benton County, Arkansas*. Bentonville, AR: Benton County Historical Society, 1993.

Black, J. Dickson. *History of Benton County, 1836–1936*. Little Rock, AR: International Graphics Industries, 1975.

Bland, Gaye K. *History of Rogers*. Unpublished. Rogers, AR: Rogers Historical Museum, 1993.

Brown, Walter L. *Our Arkansas*. Third edition. Austin, TX: Steck-Vaughn Company, 1969.

Caywood, Zoe Medlin and Carol J. Lisle. *Arkansas Celebration Cookbook*. War Eagle, AR: War Eagle Cooks, 1990.

Chapman, Dennis. *Trail of Tears, Gateway to Maysville*. Pea Ridge, AR: Benton County Bicentennial Committee, 1976.

Dougan, Michael B. *Arkansas Odyssey, The Saga of Arkansas from Prehistoric Times to Present*. Little Rock, AR: Rose Publishing Company, Inc., 1994.

Earngey, Bill and Ross Sackett, ed. asst. *Arkansas Roadsides, A Guidebook for the State*. Little Rock, AR: East Mountain Press in association with August House Publishers, 1987.

Hanson, Gerald T. and Carl H. Moneyhon. *Historical Atlas of Arkansas*. Norman, OK and London: University of Oklahoma Press, 1989.

Hough, Cass S. *It's a Daisy!* Rogers, AR: Victor Comptometer Corporation, 1976.

Johnson, Ben F. III. *Arkansas in Modern America 1930–1999*. Fayetteville, AR: The University of Arkansas Press, 2000.

McCarthy, James H., Richard McCarthy, and Carol McCarthy. *Arkansas' Past*. Jackson, CA: Conceptual Productions, 1996, 2000.

Magruder, Frank Abbott. *American Government: A Consideration or the Problems of Democracy*. Boston: Allyn and Bacon, 1942.

McKnight and Johnson. *The Arkansas Story*. Oklahoma City, OK: Harlow Publishing Co., 1956, 1960.

Moore, George. *The Gold Mines of Benton County*. Rogers, AR: F&M South Bank.

Ogg, Frederic A. and P. Orman Ray. *Introduction to American Government*. New York: D. Appleton-Century Company, 1945.

Oliver, M.E. *Old Mills of the Ozarks*. Point Lookout, MO: S of O Press, The School of the Ozarks, 1971.

Riegel, Robert E. *America Moves West*. Revised edition. New York: Henry Holt and Company, Inc., 1947.

Rogers Historical Museum. *A Walking Tour of Downtown Rogers*. Rogers, AR: Rogers Historical Museum, 1993.

Shinn, Josiah H. *Pioneers and Makers of Arkansas*. Baltimore: Genealogical Publishing Company, 1967.

Smith, Maggie Aldridge. *Simon Sager Celebration*. Siloam Springs, AR: The Simon Sager Press (A Cabincraft Book), 1986.

Steele, Phillip W. *Butterfield Run Through the Ozarks*. Springdale, AR: Heritage Publishing, n.d.

Steele, Phillip W. and Steve Cottrell. *Civil War in the Ozarks*. Gretna, LA: Pelican Publishing Company, 2000.

Steele, Phillip. *Gold in the Ozark? The Ozarks Mountaineer*, Vol. 32, Nos. 4 and 5, 1984.

Williams, C. Fred, S. Charles Bolton, Carl H. Moneyhon, and LeRoy T. Williams, eds. *A Documentary History of Arkansas*. Fayetteville, AR: University of Arkansas Press, 1984.

ADDITIONAL SOURCES

In addition to their regular coverage of historical events, the following special newspaper editions and copies of the following periodicals and magazines are particularly informative about the history of Rogers and the Ozark area:

Rogers Daily News, 15 February 1936

Rogers Daily News, 28 August 1956

Arkansas Gazette, 22 October 1967

Sunday News (Daily News), 29 February 1976

Daily News, 29 June 1976

Northwest Arkansas Morning News, 28 May 1981

Northwest Arkansas Morning News, 25 May 1986

Diamond Jubilee Souvenir Program, Presenting Rogerama, History of Rogers, 1881–1956, 1956

Benton County Pioneer, Rogers Diamond Jubilee Edition, August 1956 (and all issues)

The Ozarks Mountaineer, Kirbyville, Missouri (all issues)

INDEX